AF192404

Thomas Wanninger
Critique of Inner Leadership
A Conception of Defensibility in Democracy

Critique of Inner Leadership

A Conception of Defensibility in Democracy

Thomas Wanninger

2024

Carola Hartmann Miles-Verlag Berlin

Bibliographic information published by the German National Library
The German National Library lists this publication in the Deutsche Nationalbibliografie; detailed bibliographic data are available on the Internet at http://dnb.dnb.de.

© 2024 Carola Hartmann Miles-Verlag, Berlin
www.miles-verlag.jimdo.com
E-mail: miles-verlag@t-online.de

Production: Libri Plureos GmbH, Friedensallee 273, 22763 Hamburg

Translation, including all quotes unless otherwise indicated, by Juliane Roß, OTL

Printed in Germany

ISBN 978-3-96776-082-8

To my father

Alois Wanninger
Captain (retired)

Prologue to the English edition

World War II had an immediate impact on the historical evolution of the Bundeswehr's Inner Leadership. It placed the national identity of Germany to the test - a test that continues to this day. The government that led Germany into World War II in 1939 was not predetermined; it was elected. Not only did the Germans retain a deep mistrust of authority and the military, but also of themselves for many decades. Inner Leadership can be understood as the practice of counteracting this unease with democratic regulations. For instance, the Regulations on Military Complaints, the Ordinance on Superiors, and the jurisdiction of civilian criminal courts for military disciplinary proceedings date back to the early days of the Bundeswehr. In addition, there is a parliamentary reservation of authority for armed forces operations and a general authority that, by international standards, possesses relatively limited authority.

A second origin of the term Inner Leadership is the Prussian tradition of handling its soldiers "decently." This unwritten law developed its effect in significant portions of the Wehrmacht but was gradually supplanted by National Socialism's disregard. This has resulted in the Inner Leaderships' tendency toward codified orders since the inception of the Bundeswehr. This has, 70 years after the founding of the Bundeswehr, resulted in widespread ossification of formulas and concepts, thereby calling into doubt the vitality of Inner Leadership itself. Organizing a revitalization here through the multi-perspective topic of "diversity" is audacious, given that the focus of Inner Leadership must be the concrete leadership performance in the soldiers! General Graf v. Kielmansegg's 1971 definition that spears are constructed on the point, not the shaft, is legitimate.

Thus concludes this concise historical introduction to Inner Leadership, which requires classification outside of Germany. - Gratitude for democracy is likely the most significant source of Inner Leadership, though. This attitude toward the state and community will always be essential for the soldiers of today's generation. That is our raison d'être! This third origin has the additional advantage of lacking the specific characteristics of German history and being able to demonstrate the principles of Inner Leadership for all armed forces in democratic nations. This book focuses almost exclusively on the third foundation of Inner Leadership, making it particularly suitable for international presentation. The Bundeswehr clarified its tradition to the Wehrmacht in 2018; as an organization, it is not worthy of tradition. As such, as a negative template, it is incapable of imparting a notion of Inner Leadership. This notion must be derived from democratic principles, which Germany and many other nations share.

In terms of the humanities, according to my interpretation, these systematic considerations have their foundation in the era of "Deutschen Idealismus" of the late 18th century, which was significantly influenced by the French Revolution. Schiller, Kant, and Hegel are the influential authors of this era. This volume emanates from this world of thought, along with the military imprint of the German army (infantry) and an acute awareness of current events.

Lieutenant Colonel Juliane Roß approached me immediately following the publication of the German edition of "Kritik der Inneren Führung" and requested the English translation for her use in the Canadian Department of National Defence.

Any armed forces that wish to achieve success for nation, alliance, and democracy must be firmly rooted in its nation and its soldiers. It can only accomplish this if it remembers its mission, its ideals, and each individual combatant.

Regensburg, July 20, 2023

Dr. Thomas Wanninger

Content

Bad witnesses are people's eyes and ears when the soul does not understand their language.
Heraclitus of Ephesus[1]

[1] Heraklit, *Fragmente*, Bd. 14 (Zürich und München: Artemis & Winkler, 2007).

1   What is a critique? - An introduction

The concepts of individuality and freedom are highly valued and can be rightfully claimed by all citizens within a democratic nation. For several decades, the notion of individualistic approaches to personal decision-making and professional growth has been widely accepted. In contrast, the realm of the military is characterized by a nuanced and ambiguous nature. At first sight, individuality is superseded by uniformity, and freedom is relinquished in favor of authority. The utilization of weaponry, encompassing acts of lethal force, exceeds conventional cognitive understanding. One could pose the question: Can a democratic system descend to such uncivilized depths without ultimately dismantling itself, seemingly contradicting its fundamental principles?

Germany is home to a diverse range of philosophical paradigms that establish a valid framework for individuals or collectives. The various personal philosophies are inherently susceptible to alteration. In order to effectively comprehend and interpret sensory stimuli, it is imperative for individuals to maintain a receptive state of mind, with their visual and auditory faculties attuned. Additionally, the soul (*psyche*), traditionally regarded as the locus of consciousness and introspection, assumes the responsibility of deciphering the intricate language embedded within these sensory impressions. What constitutes significance or importance? What changes are necessary and in what direction should the state's development occur? The examination of personal and social inquiries is a recurring occurrence observed in daily newspaper perusal.

Since the outbreak of the conflict in Ukraine, the prominence of external security has resurfaced as a significant concern within the realm of societal progress. The role of *defensibility* as a fundamental principle within the democratic state is a topic of growing discussion. This discourse shapes a philosophy that subsequently impacts the behavior of both individuals and collectives. The compatibility between defensibility with arms and democratic peace values appears to be contradictory. This book aims to demonstrate the contrary. Simultaneously, the objective is to provide a systematic elucidation of how a military force can be perceived within a democratic framework, thereby ensuring that democracy extends beyond the barracks gate.

The justification for the use of force and the demand of citizen for military service must be established. The apprehension of potential adversaries is a subjective emotion rather than a valid rationale. Covenants represent a legally binding commitment rather than serving as an internal rationale. The Bundeswehr, commonly referred to as the German Armed Forces, relies on the democratic ethos of Inner Leadership as a foundation for its self-defense capabilities. Like other democratic armed forces, it is founded on the principles delineated in its internal constitution.

The concept of Inner Leadership within the Bundeswehr encompasses the soul of soldiers, as well as the fundamental essence of the German nation, to which every member of the military is dedicated in upholding the principles of law and freedom. The originators of the concept of Inner Leadership can be attributed with the establishment of these fundamental principles. In order to ensure that the German Armed Forces no longer bore resemblance to the former Wehrmacht, it became imperative to establish clear regulations and protocols that continue to shape the Bundeswehr in the present day. This was essential to bestow upon the Bundeswehr the necessary legitimacy to actively defend democratic principles.

The aforementioned merit, particularly attributed to three German Generals Wolf von Baudissin, Ulrich de Maizière, and Johann Adolf Graf von Kielmansegg, is gradually becoming outdated, potentially giving rise to the perception of a divergence in both substance and linguistic expression. According to Friedrich Schiller, a renowned German author and philosopher, it can be asserted with accuracy that an individual possesses dual citizenship in both the temporal dimension and the political entity commonly referred to as the state. [2] The temporal distance between the present and the 1950s/1960s, during which the Bundeswehr and Inner Leadership were established, further accentuates the distinction between these two realms. All three of the mentioned generals belong to a long-ago age and could be thought of as great-grandfathers to the soldiers who serve today in units and formations.[3] Consequently, the individuals commonly referred to as the founding fathers of Inner Leadership have become absent as present-day witnesses. The direct connection they had through shared life experiences has been broken, releasing them from direct observation and limiting them to photographic records and mental frameworks.

The temporal distance and the absence of systematic approaches have played a role in prompting the need for a revitalization of Inner Leadership or the development of a fresh narrative by authors like Sven Lange, Nicolas Holz, Uwe Hartmann, and Marcel Bohnert.[4] I would like to explicitly endorse this proposition. - Hence, it is imperative to initiate a discussion regarding the nature of this narrative in the preliminary considerations, as this inquiry provides guidance and ultimately delves into the essence of this book.

---

[2] Cf. Friedrich Schiller, *Über die ästhetische Erziehung des Menschen in einer Reihe von Briefen* (Stuttgart: Reclam, 1993), p.5.

[3] Sven Lange, „Fit für das 21. Jahrhundert: Warum die Konzeption der Inneren Führung eine neue Meistererzählung benötigt", hg. von Uwe et al Hartmann, *Jahrbuch Innere Führung 2020*, 2020, p.31.

[4] The authors mentioned will be further examined and supported with corresponding evidence throughout the book.

The Bundeswehr has been effectively positioned for several decades owing to its implementation of the principle of Inner Leadership. The integration of compliance rules into the Inner Leadership of companies was a protracted process. Several other government agencies exhibit a complete absence of Inner Leadership. The Bundeswehr frequently lacks awareness of the advantages it provides in this regard.

To retain and reinforce this advantage, the thesis contends that the Bundeswehr must adopt a concept of democratic military service that has previously been lacking.

I.

A narrative possesses the potential to be a compelling and captivating account that engrosses the reader or listener.[5] These narrative endeavors to establish a connection with the individual and, in accordance with the principles of effective persuasion, initially aims to establish an emotional bond (*conciliare*). Subsequently, the individual is provided with guidance and knowledge (*docere*), which is presented in an engaging manner to evoke a sense of delight (*delectare*). This approach is widely appreciated as it satisfies the innate human desire to acquire novel and meaningful information. Upon reaching a state characterized by openness and curiosity, the transition to prompting the listener to introspect is a natural progression (*movere*). This prompts a sense of restlessness and initiates a state of movement within the listener (*agitare*), ultimately leading to the speaker exerting influence through the listener. - An instance of this narrative form can be observed in the traditional oration delivered by a field commander prior to a battle. Another notable example is the renowned speech delivered by British Prime Minister Churchill on May 10, 1940, aimed at bolstering the determination to defend his nation.[6] - Nevertheless, the objective of this book is not simply to reiterate preexisting information regarding Inner Leadership.

A different method of creating a fresh narrative would be to investigate the *capabilities of Inner Leadership* instead of depending just on reliable sources and relevant books. Instead, one could engage in a *comprehensive reevaluation of Inner Leadership from its fundamental principles*. In what manner can it exert an impact? On the other hand, how might it appear in the context of serving during both peace and war? In order to seek answers to these two analogous inquiries, reliance solely on personal impressions is inadequate. Instead, a comprehensive framework must be established, necessitating the integration of the historical intellectual discourse within the cultural domain. However, it is justifiable to employ the term "narrative" in the context of these humanities deliberations, as the axioms presented in this publication have their foundation in the rhetoric of the French mathematician and philosopher Blaise Pascal (1623-1662).

---

[5] Marcus Tullius Cicero, *De oratore / Vom Redner*, übers. von H. Reclam Merklin (Stuttgart: Merklin, H., Reclam, 1986), pp.114f.

[6] This is his famous short speech to the House of Commons three days after his appointment as prime minister. "Blood, sweat and tears," would cost the defense of the war. The genius of this speech is its brevity, obvious honesty, and use of the right terms. The German linguist Wolf Schneider (1925-2022) has repeatedly pointed out that the use of *old and short terms* is most effective, which is true for all languages. Cf. Wolf Schneider, *Deutsch für Kenner. Die neue Stilkunde.*, 8. Aufl. (München/Zürich: Piper, 2003), pp.61-64.

The method of *highlighting capabilities* was already employed in the primary works of Immanuel Kant (1724-1804), the most important German-speaking philosopher from Königsberg/East Prussia. To accomplish this objective, Kant authored three critical works that delve into the faculties of the human mind, moral principles, and the faculty of judgment.

In order to comprehensively examine the capabilities and justifications of Inner Leadership, a *critique* is required, which entails presenting a systematic evaluation of its capabilities and constraints. Many attempts have been made to determine what Inner Leadership is all about, mostly motivated by the practical necessity of creating an instruction manual, handbook, or teaching tool.[7] As a result, these efforts tend to remain scattered because the core of inner leadership, and especially the seemingly important question: "What is Inner Leadership?" is difficult to define. It should be noted that the preceding definitions of Inner Leadership are not necessarily incorrect, nor should the ideas and perspectives that have been expressed and contemplated over the course of several decades be dismissed as absurd. Only the contents are not based on themselves and are merely an additive sequence, which is also often called the "DNA of the Bundeswehr". The aforementioned "content-related hereditary information" are merely components of Inner Leadership, lacking inherent impact or sufficient rationale to justify their indispensability. The mere existence and apparent plausibility of something does not suffice as an argument or a valid conceptual understanding.

Furthermore, it is imperative that all theoretical concepts are both *identifiable* and *applicable* within the context of everyday military operations. Most importantly, these theories should be *actively embraced* and implemented by troops. Regarding the concept of Inner Leadership, there is a discernible undercurrent of discontent present in this context. Authors who have explored this phenomenon in their literary works will be part within this book. - In the field of biology, the DNA sequence serves as a means of uncovering the fundamental components of life. However, it is important to note that DNA itself does not possess any inherent life or knowledge regarding the origins of amino acid activity. It can be seen in the context of Inner Leadership that the development of effect is dependent on the use of reasoning and, most importantly, liveliness. The DNA in and of itself lacks functionality.

Therefore, a critical reevaluation of Inner Leadership requires a purposeful break from traditional literature and an exploration of a genuine logic that is not only shaped by the early Bundeswehr's formative experiences but also conforms to a necessary humanities standard. Thus far, the Inner Leadership

---

[7] Cf. Reinhold Janke, „Innere Führung verstehen, gestalten und erleben.", *IF 1/23. Zeitschrift für Innere Führung*, 2023, p.43.

of the Bundeswehr has shown shortcomings that have had serious ramifications and prevented the principles of Inner Leadership from truly evolving further.

The current depiction of Inner Leadership appears to primarily consist of a factual narrative. The German regulations of Inner Leadership exhibit a notable density of nouns.[8] The determining factor, however, does not lie in the desire for comprehensiveness, but rather in the internal preparedness and willingness to embrace a democratic nation, which ultimately must also be safeguarded through defensive military means.

This has to be explained; it is not done with mere stipulations and definitions. This imposes a certain obligation on the currently responsible generations, and it can give the impression that it takes almost as long to explain democracy as it did to implement it decades earlier. - In German history, it took three attempts in the years 1848, 1919 and 1949 (West) / 1990 (East) to reach the democracy that today offers us the opportunity to raise ourselves from subservient to citizens.

The narrative surrounding freedom centers on the internal disposition exhibited by individuals who identify as proponents of democracy in relation to their nation.[9] Numerous scholarly works and regulatory documents pertaining to Inner Leadership predominantly emphasize the objectives and contents of this concept, rather than its underlying disposition. The aforementioned concepts are condensed and organized into four categories: legitimation, integration, motivation, and shaping the internal order. Upon closer examination of the concept of legitimation, it becomes evident that it encompasses various aspects, such as "ethical, legal, political, and social justifications for engaging in military action[10]". Under these aspects, one can envision a multitude of possibilities. The legal framework remains the sole stable and well-defined component in this context.

Additionally, this book will address the ethical rationale behind military service. The establishment of a robust basis for the armed forces is imperative, encompassing not only a solid legal framework but also a favorable disposition from both the soldiers and society towards the armed forces.

In order to develop a fresh narrative, it is imperative to generate novel ideas that, as the conclusion of the book will reveal, bear numerous resemblances

---

[8] Cf. Bundesministerium der Verteidigung, *Innere Führung. Selbstverständnis und Führungskultur. A-2600/1* (Bonn, 2008), Paras 301 - 316.

[9] The term "inner attitude" hasbecome a difficult terminology in the Bundeswehr. In April 2017, former Minister of Defense Ursula von der Leyen believed that the Bundeswehr as a whole had an "attitude problem". For the purposes of understanding this book, her statements can be omitted without loss of content.

[10] op. cit.,BMVg, *Innere Führung. Selbstverständnis und Führungskultur. A-2600/1.*, para. 401.

to the principles espoused by the progenitors of Inner Leadership. This encompasses both recently published and previously unexplored literature within the Bundeswehr. This book posits that adopting this approach is a promising mean of effectively establishing the principles and objectives of Inner Leadership up until the present moment, thereby transitioning from a mere *listing of ideas* to a *coherent and organized narrative.*

The pathway to a comprehensive narrative that encompasses and unifies Inner Leadership as a framework is rooted in a spiritual receptiveness and, firmly grounded in the tradition of philosophy. This spiritual openness serves as a contrasting element, enabling the justification of all other aspects and illuminating them in a favorable manner. In this manner, the concept of Inner Leadership encompasses both physical and moral dimensions as it emphasizes the importance of acceptance and voluntary dedication that arise from a foundation of individual freedom.

This rationale can only be situated within the framework of the humanities, as historical and empirical methodology is limited to assessing and analyzing existing phenomena. However, in this context, individuals are limited to relying solely on established facts and information that have developed over time. These facts and contents remain unexplained in their inherent meaning and lack the ability to provide reasoning on their own. It is entirely outside the scope of historical empirical research and measurability to determine why and how anything should be.

If the new approach to Inner Leadership does not encompass historical or empirical aspects, it can be seen as a negative definition that sets a boundary on the potential achievements of this book. The statement fails to acknowledge the potential positive outcomes. - The subject matter pertains to a *critique* in the traditional sense, as previously stated. However, the act of writing a critique is commonly perceived in informal discourse as the act of identifying and highlighting areas of weakness. The text can be interpreted in an alternative manner, specifically in its inherent sense as the *practice of discernment and differentiation.* Therefore, it is imperative to establish clarity and precision in language, as well as logical organization, in the process of evaluating and making judgments. The establishment of a revitalized Inner Leadership is predicated upon a *foundational framework that ensures the endurance of timeless correctness.*

After addressing the critique, attention can be directed towards the core principles of Inner Leadership. The aforementioned objective has been designated in the introductory citation attributed to Heraclitus: *Enlightenment* of the soul.[11] It possesses the capability to identify and arrange.

However, it is necessary to have *foundations that are no longer in need of any justification*. These will become the axioms of Inner Leadership. Whoever knows them and, moreover, identifies them in every days troop activity can feel with a delicate sense and democratic consciousness what no study or historical safeguard can ever bring about: a unique *understanding at the critical juncture of making a decision*.

---

[11] It is widely acknowledged that the extant corpus of Heraclitus of Ephesus consists solely of fragmentary remains, thereby posing challenges for scholarly investigation. Nevertheless, it is the utilization of quotations and concise expressions that appears to have set Heraclitus apart even in his own time during the 6th century BC. It is reasonable to adhere to the perspectives of Hans-Georg Gadamer in this context. (See Hans-Georg Gadamer, *Der Anfang des Wissens* (Stuttgart: Reclam, 1999)., p. 14f) Heraclitus' textual compilations did not possess the nature of a doctrinal composition, in contrast to his contemporary Parmenides. Instead, these ideas serve as the central foundation of his thought, characterized by the integration of diverse elements, the recognition of opposing forces, the equitable treatment of differences, and the inherent need for interpretation. The fragments serve as the focal point of attention, around which the entire "mind map of thinking" had to evolve. The act of interpretation, as undertaken by the thoughtful reader, constituted an integral aspect of Heraclites work and was aligned with his intended purpose. The significance of his thought process holds relevance within the context of Inner Leadership. The perceived paradox concerning the coexistence of democratic freedom and the utilization of force by a democratic military has already been examined and discussed. The cognitive entity known as the soul, despite its inherent capacity for thought, has the ability to establish a cohesive whole. The Milesians regarded the soul as the essence of respiration. Conversely, Heraclitus perceived the soul as an enigmatic concept of limitless potentiality, within which the rational soul operates. Op. cit. Gadamer. p. 13

II.

The primary focus should now be on a narrative that is substantiated and organized through critical observation. Why do we serve? What societal benefits and values make such acts significant and valuable? What philosophical or ethical perspectives justify personal sacrifices in the pursuit of service? What justifications exist for the legitimate use of force and the acceptance of potential violence in service-related contexts? Only those who are well-versed - and in extreme cases, bulletproof - truly grasp the purpose of armed forces in a democratic context. However, this comprehension must arise organically from a deep-seated recognition of both personal autonomy and accountability, to the extent that it no longer necessitates any form of rationalization. It is critical to devote significant time and effort to thorough investigation of the subject matter, rather than depending merely on superficial and polished articulations of ethical, legal, political, and social notions. The mere addition of these concepts does not create a full comprehension or grasp of the subject topic.

The pivotal role in this context will be attributed to the notion of *axioms*, as expounded by the mathematician and rhetorician Blaise Pascal (1623-1662). Axioms, being *intuitive principles that necessitate no validation*, not only delineate the substance, but also serve as its justification. Within the intricate framework of Inner Leadership, a sense of cohesion can be fostered among the various constituent elements. *Commitment can only emerge from this particular connection.* By adopting this approach, it becomes feasible to transition from a mere compilation of information (*convolute*)[12] to a *concept* that is substantiated and grounded in solid foundations.

Since its establishment, the concept of Inner Leadership within the Bundeswehr has comprised regulations and insights that are largely plausible and have gained historical significance. Up until now, there has been an incorrect designation of this notion as the concept of Inner Leadership. It is not unexpected that plausibilities shift dramatically over time.

The constant effort to adapt Inner Leadership to changing plausibilities is a weakness that has existed since the beginnings of the Bundeswehr. This cannot succeed without first clarifying a timeless concept of defensiveness in democracy, because there are no viable arguments.

---

[12] The confrontation of the pair of terms "Convolute vs Concept" will come up again and again in the course of the considerations. Today, the term "Convolute" is mainly used in auctions, where for a certain amount of money, for example, a bundle of used watches can be bought, from which the buyer can choose the most suitable item.

To make matters worse, the robust arguments - which the axioms of Inner Leadership will prove to be - are lacking in an area of social life that can be particularly challenging for citizens. It is about nothing less than national defence, where life and health must be jeopardized in an emergency and state sovereignty, the rights, and freedoms of the German people are at issue.

III.

The first stage in conceptualizing is to investigate why such a narrative is required. The introduction kicked off the topic, which will be expanded on in the preliminary thoughts that follow. Ernst-Wolfgang Böckenförde's views, a renowned German academic in the fields of constitutional and administrative law, philosophy of law, and a former judge at Germany's Federal Constitutional Court, can also be linked to Pascal's concept of axioms.

The focus of systematics should revolve around the humanistic underpinnings of Inner Leadership, which is established through explicit guiding inquiries. The authors and philosophers Friedrich Schiller, Georg Wilhelm Friedrich Hegel, and Emanuel Levinas will provide significant contributions in this context.[13]

The determination of five *axioms* is based on the content derived from the preliminary considerations and the systematics. To establish their affiliation with the tradition of Inner Leadership, it can be demonstrated that Wolf von Baudissin, Ulrich de Maizière, and Johann Adolf Graf von Kielmansegg have essentially aligned themselves with it.

The concluding remarks seek to offer a concise perspective on the potential impact of this book on the Bundeswehr and forces from other democratic nations.

To maintain readability, it is advisable to alternate between two distinct linguistic and argumentative styles within the book. In the context of scientific discourse, as demonstrated in the preceding introduction, it is customary to identify, expound upon, and assess relevant scholarly works. However, it is important to acknowledge the justification of employing a journalistic style as it allows for straightforward observations and practical life examples, providing the mind with a sense of respite before the subsequent quotation once again captures full attention.

---

[13] The systematics of Inner Leadership thus refers to an essay published in the "Inner Leadership 2021/22 Yearbook". Cf. Thomas Wanninger, „Mögliche Grundlegung einer erneuerten Inneren Führung für die Bundeswehr", hg. von Uwe Hartmann, *Jahrbuch Innere Führung 2021/22*, 2022, pp. 375-385.

2   Preparatory considerations

2.1 The Road to the Axioms of Inner Leadership

In the absence of a comprehensive exposition on the subject of Inner Leadership, it becomes imperative to examine its present status and developments pertaining to Inner Leadership.

The inquiry persists: Is an adjunct to Inner Leadership indispensable? Undoubtedly, a substantial body of German literature has been amassed over time and progress is being made. In situations where obstacles arise, there exist mechanisms, specialized knowledge, and, if required, hierarchical systems to rectify the situation and enhance performance.

Nevertheless, the focal point is not merely the compatibility of structures and the subsequent functionality of processes within the armed forces. The necessity for a new narrative for the Bundeswehr is evident, as there seems to be a lack of clarity regarding its desired form and content. The absence of guidance raises the question of our desire for it in this particular manner. The mere engagement in activities and the generation of outcomes cannot serve as a substitute for addressing this inquiry.

The narrative constructed in response should be supported by valid justifications and be defensible in nature. The introduction has already provided preliminary ideas, and it is worth noting that Inner Leadership can *transition from a convolute of information to a framework of interconnected understandings that no longer necessitate further explanation.* The purpose of these observations is to address a clear inadequacy of Inner Leadership by consolidating various commonly used terms such as citizens in uniform, spiritual armament, DNA of the Bundeswehr, spiritual heritage of Europe, primacy of politics, principles and interests of German security and defence policy, constitutional mandate, liberal and pluralistic social order, living in tolerance and diversity, and so on.

In recent years, there has been a lack of initiative in formulating a novel narrative for Inner Leadership. On the contrary, there is a prevailing perception that it is entirely antiquated and ill-suited for operational missions, to the extent that it could conceivably be eradicated. The primary priority of an armed forces is to ensure its functionality, and any additional intellectual weight, should be eliminated.[14] The persistent presence of contradictory elements, which have manifested themselves since the publication of the Himmerode

---

[14] This opinion is primarily held by Marcel Bohnert. Cf. Marcel Bohnert, *Innere Führung auf dem Prüfstand* (Hamburg: Deutscher Veteranen Verlag, 2017), pp.35-39.

Memorandum[15], remains unresolved. It is true that the idea of Innere Fuehung reached a dead end a long time ago and has frequently been seen primarily from a historical perspective. The overall concept of Inner Leadership is adversely affected by a deficiency in dynamism and widespread acceptance. This raises the valid question of whether conceptual methods exist, as it appears that the prevailing trend has been one of fair compromises rather than unique conceptual frameworks. In the context of soccer, it can be argued that Inner Leadership often aligns with a traditional game concept and obsolete game technique. It is arguable that attending the World Cup alongside Sepp Herberger (a former legendary German soccer coach)[16], given his limited ability to perceive the trajectory of the ball in contemporary gameplay, may not be advisable.

The conceptual inadequacy becomes further evident with the absence of individuals who held a deep personal connection to Inner Leadership and have since retired. This was already highlighted by Uwe Hartmann[17] in 2007: "Where can the leaders of Unna be found, who actively engage in advocating for their cause[18]", Hartmann rightly asks. According to Marie-Luise Strack-Zimmermann, the chairwoman of the defense committee in the Bundestag, there is a need for "increased clarity and reduced empty phrases in the realm of generalship[19]". This assertion can indeed be substantiated; however, it is important to consider the circumstances surrounding the generals who can be placed in retirement without justification - a practice that has already been

---

[15] In October 1950, a conference took place at the Himmerod Abby in close vicinity of Trier, when former German officers convened to strategize and make preparations for the rearmament of Germany. This initiative was undertaken within the context of the European Defence Community (EDC) and aimed at integrating Germany into the Western sphere, under the leadership of the first German Chancellor, Konrad Adenauer. The outcome of the discussion led to the creation of the Himmeroder Denkschrift, which featured a concise yet influential section discussing the "internal structure" of the military. The EDC project had a failure in 1952 mostly due to France's involvement. However, it is noteworthy that the component pertaining to the "internal structure" developed by Wolf von Baudissin is widely regarded as the genesis of Inner Leadership. This particular section was subsequently integrated into the newly established Bundeswehr in 1955.

[16] Sepp Herberger (1897-1977) is a legendary German soccer coach who lead his country to the 1954 World Cup in Bern. The "Miracle of Bern" with a 3:2 victory over Hungary was an emotionally significant turning point for Germany to be able to turn inward to the "Miracle of Democracy" in a positive frame of mind and have hope for a bright future after the war.

[17] Dr. Uwe Hartmann (born in 1962) currently serves as the Director of Education at the Centre for Military History and Social Sciences of the Bundeswehr in Potsdam. He has been an expert on the Bundeswehr's Inner Leadership for many years.

[18] Uwe Hartmann, *Innere Führung. Erfolge und Defizite der Führungsphilosophie für die Bundeswehr* (Berlin: Miles-Verlag, 2007), p114.

[19] Marie-Agnes Strack-Zimmermann, „Wünsche mir mehr Klarheit und weniger Geschwurbel der Generalität" (www.WELT.de, Januar 2022).

observed on multiple occasions. This condition, lacking any discernible professional inadequacy, is deemed unsustainable from the perspective of Inner Leadership. There is a prevalent and justified expectation that Inner Leadership ought to be universally applicable to both military personnel and civilian staff, with an uncompromising adherence to this principle extending to the leadership as well.

One prominent illustration of the persistence of antiquated notions is the widely invoked concept of the "citizen in uniform,"[20] which frequently arises in discussions surrounding the principles of Inner Leadership. The original meaning of the term is clearly outdated, as evidenced by its historical origins. Prior to the establishment of the Bundeswehr, soldiers in Germany were subject to a restricted set of rights. When this alteration occurred, individuals appropriately referred to the concept of the "citizen in uniform." Nonetheless, it is critical to recognize that the current issue does not concern the rejection of granting the soldier the rights of a citizen. However, it is related to the decreasing willingness of many people in the public to temporarily undertake the commitments associated with military enlistment.[21] The military service that citizens have enjoyed is a general right since the French Revolution[22]; what remains is largely unfamiliar to the majority of individuals. The experience of living in a uniformed environment primarily constitutes a

---

[20] Cf. Wehrgesetz des Deutschen Reiches in its 1935-1944 version, 26, Abs. 1 through 3. The prohibition on soldiers engaging in political activity extended to the NSDAP. In the Reich, the right to vote and partake in elections was suspended. To join organizations within and outside of the Wehrmacht, soldiers needed permission from their superiors. But not only political and social citizenship rights were restricted for Wehrmacht members. Section 27 interfered directly with private life; the soldier's (disciplinary) superior had to be requested if he was permitted to marry. The Bundeswehr was initially unaware of these restrictions.

[21] Timo Graf, „Zwischen Anspruch und Wirklichkeit: Wie steht es um die Bündnistreue in der Bevölkerung.", hg. von U. et al Hartmann, *Jahrbuch Innere Führung 2021/22.*, 2022, pp.129ff.

[22] The informal chairman of the Directory, Paul de Barras (1755-1829), assumes a significant role in this context. There is a significant dearth of information available in German regarding an intriguing individual in military history, whose political influence was mostly observed during the transitional period between the Jacobin regime and the ascension of Napoleon.

There is a dearth of knowledge regarding Napoleon's assumption of power in the German context. The sole biography of notable value is authored by Arnold Steiniger in 1953. It is not well recognized that the vernacular designation of the conscript army, commonly referred to as Barras, may be traced back to its association with him.

fundamental entitlement, while simultaneously representing an obligatory commitment for those who lack enthusiasm towards. [23]

The discourse surrounding the "state within the state[24]" during the initial period of the Bundeswehr in Weimar[25] is now considered obsolete. In contemporary times, it is imperative for both the state and public opinion to establish a clear understanding of their association with the Bundeswehr. This means analyzing whether the Bundeswehr remains significant within the German nation's ethos, and whether it connects with the sentiments of its people, particularly in relation to the pressing worries that constantly arise regarding the future. The annexation of Crimea in 2014 and the subsequent conflict in Ukraine has elicited significant shifts in public sentiment. Initially, the situation was regarded as a humanitarian crisis, but it has subsequently been reevaluated as a military predicament. Nevertheless, the extent of unforeseen developments and their potential implications for Germany's preparedness and defensive capabilities are yet to be determined. German security interests and loyalty to the alliance have received limited attention until recently.[26]

It is evident that this development is incongruent with the principles and objectives of Inner Leadership. In her essay, Dr. Meike Wanner, a senior researcher at the Centre for Military History and Social Sciences of the Armed Forces, perceptively observes that "the advocates of Inner Leadership harbored legitimate apprehensions regarding the potential resurgence of a

---

[23] Occasionally, however, the citizen is also constrained by the Bundeswehr procurement system because it is unable to purchase uniforms for the citizen. "Bundeswehr soldiers in Lithuania lack jackets and underwear. The poor equipment of the Bundeswehr has been discussed for years. Defense Commissioner Eva Högl has noted with dismay that the troops in the NATO mission in the northeast lack the most basic necessities." Spiegel online 25.02.2022. Translated by the author.

[24] After World War I, the position of the Reichswehr (1921-1935), which was partially outside the law and renamed the Wehrmacht in 1935, was a design defect in the German constitution of 1919.

[25] If the concept of a "state within a state" continues to persist in contemporary times, it is not observable within the Bundeswehr. The churches, with their establishment of their own labour regulations and the potential for internal resolution of criminal offences, are subject to more scrutiny in this context. This principle is also applicable to any form of internal jurisdiction, such as those observed in major sports associations. From its inception, the Bundeswehr has intentionally refrained from implementing a militia jurisdiction. Civilian courts are responsible for adjudicating all military offences.

[26] Timo Graf provides concrete figures and an even more differentiated analysis of this in the Yearbook Inner Leadership 2021/22, Graf, „Zwischen Anspruch und Wirklichkeit: Wie steht es um die Bündnistreue in der Bevölkerung." pp. 129-155.

disconnection between society, politics, and the military.[27]" Regrettably, a gap has indeed arisen, albeit in a manner distinct from the initial concerns within the Bundeswehr. Specifically, this gap does not stem from an intellectual and legal division within the armed forces, but rather from societal perceptions that have relegated the state's exclusive authority over the use of force to a morally compromised position. Executive institutions in charge of external security are widely regarded to be influenced by a defective mentality, as it is argued that using violence to resolve problems is no longer a viable method in modern times.[28] The United Nations, along with other state alliances and the concept of "Change through Trade" were anticipated to yield significant results.[29] The outcomes and implications of an ineffective and defenseless making policy are currently indeterminable.

However, the game of Inner Leadership, akin to the analogy of soccer, remains pertinent, albeit necessitating a modified approach. Individuals who hold the belief that they can function effectively without the concept of Inner Leadership ought to examine the circumstances prevalent in other military forces that are able to operate without its implementation.[30]

Concentrating on the axiom of Inner Leadership as the basis of a new narrative, on the other hand, has a certain allure that needs to be filled with life after a humanities-based consideration. In addition to advocating for a shift from simple *convolute* towards a concept, it is imperative to emphasize the importance of revitalization. This revitalization can only be achieved by effectively incorporating axioms that resonate with social and military-oriented experiences, thereby enhancing the overall impact of the discourse. The

---

[27] Meike Wanner, „Innere Führung – Philosophie der Streitkräfte oder bloße Anleitung zur Menschenführung?", hg. von M. Elbe, *Philosophie des Militärs*, 2022, p.155.

[28] The so-called "Manifesto for Peace" presented by Wagenknecht and Schwarzer in 2023 may be regarded as a document of this zeitgeist, which does not shy away from slurring reality. Cf.Alice Schwarzer und Sahra Wagenknecht, „Manifest für Frieden", 2023. https://www.change.org/p/manifest-f%C3%BCr-frie- den.

[29] Following the reunification of Germany in 1990, policymakers in Germany held the assumption that political systems could be altered by means of commercial connections, drawing inspiration from the Western perspective. The primary emphasis was directed against Russia and China. This concept may be deemed unsuccessful. The principal proponents of this school of thinking, which is characterized by a lack of strategic orientation, were Chancellors Schröder and Merkel, with President Steinmeier, who continues to hold office and has exerted significant influence on German foreign policy over an extended period of time.

[30] The literary works authored by Yishai Sarid, a former Israeli intelligence officer born in 1965, serve as a noteworthy illustration of both linguistic and thematic excellence. The novel "Siegerin" explores the journey of a military psychologist who grapples with the challenges posed by an army lacking Inner Leadership, as depicted in the book. The protagonist must exert much effort to address the detrimental impact that such a military organization has on its own soldiers, necessitating her resourcefulness in implementing temporary solutions.

likelihood of achieving success using language and social backgrounds from previous generations, specifically those of one's great-grandfathers, is questionable. The military troops must be the primary source of inspiration for this project. People are able to participate in the mental processes and create a new structure for their own narratives. However, the aware understanding of service operations provides a challenge and is a noteworthy achievement for the leadership. The proponents of Inner Leadership did not originate the concept, but they demonstrated intellectual courage, which contributed to their notable achievements during the period of reestablishment of the German armed forces. In contemporary times, there remains a persistent requirement for soldiers across various echelons who possess the qualities of steadfast loyalty and critical thinking, thereby engendering the trust necessary to contemplate and execute actions in accordance with the principles of Inner Leadership.[31]

2.1.1 Current literature on conceptual thinking in Inner Leadership

The Bundeswehr's official internal command is not currently engaged in the development of a concept for Inner Leadership. As a result, the focus for this study will be directed towards a carefully selected collection of current academic literature. The central emphasis lies in the *consolidation* of the enduring narrative that emerged during the mid-twentieth century.[32] The primary objective of this review methodology is to discern and analyze the fundamental conceptual components present within recent scholarly works.

The publication of "Zurück in die Zukunft" (Back to the Future) in 2021, written by Nicolas Holz, is notable for its subtitle which explicitly acknowledges that the content presented is not novel. The objective is to engage in a comprehensive analysis and enhancement of Inner Leadership through a critical reassessment of its existing components. A summary titled "Innere Führung seit der Gründung der Bundeswehr – Was können wir aus

---

[31] At this juncture, it is pertinent to bring to your attention the notable figure of Major General Berthold von Stauffenberg, within whose division staff the subsequent Inspector General Schneiderhan rendered his services. During a televised interview, Stauffenberg expressed his preference for staff officers who are willing to challenge and contradict him in situations where he may be expressing ideas or statements that lack logical or factual basis. The source "ARD, 2009" can be found on the website youtube.com. Regrettably, in practical scenarios, both within and particularly beyond the Bundeswehr, the aforementioned statement frequently holds true: 'Individuals who are unwilling to conceal my irrational actions are deemed disloyal and must be eliminated.' B. M.v Stauffenberg, „Teil 2 Porträt General Schneiderhan" (www.youtube.com ARD 2009).

[32] One notable exception is to Bohnert's diverse submissions, which will be examined individually within the context of the systematics of Inner Leadership. Hence, it is imperative to acknowledge and consider various stakeholders involved in the ongoing discourse.

Fehlentwicklungen lernen?" (Inner Leadership since the establishment of the Bundeswehr - What can we learn from misdevelopments?) is examined in the Inner Leadership 2021/22 yearbook, with a focus on the lessons that can be derived from unfavorable developments. The objective is to extract insights from the unfavorable occurrences associated with this concept. In this independent publication, Holz clearly demonstrates his proficiency by conducting a comparative examination of the evolution of official publications and regulations, commencing with the "Handbuch Innere Führung" (Manual for Inner Leadership) published by the German Ministry of Defense in 1957 and extending to the contemporary era. In a manner akin to a synoptic methodology, Holz arranges textual materials in a columnar structure[33] and discerns elements that have been disregarded but retain significance. This is evident in the concept of the "war image," which Wolf von Baudissin speaks about in the same way that he writes about the "democratic society".[34] After conducting a comprehensive analysis of the topic, Holz also raises the inquiry: "What are the effective strategies for fulfilling one's duty? [35]". The focus is mostly on the service mentality and approach, rather than the core ideas of Inner Leadership. This prompts a closer look at its essential parallels. Holz presents a discerning perspective on the fundamental principles and popular terminology linked to Inner Leadership, which are frequently presented in a simplistic and shallow fashion within German doctrines. The validity of this critical perspective is warranted in specific circumstances. According to Holz (2021), the concise version derived from the German regulation on Inner Leadership lacks a compelling narrative drive. The messages presented exhibit a deficiency in depth and substance, as they offer explanations that, while not inaccurate, are rather constrained in their breadth. The statement additionally posits that Inner Leadership must exhibit internal coherence.[36] Once again, the present discourse centers on the regrettable absence of an argumentative nature, thereby highlighting the significance of the concept of Inner Leadership. The culmination of this viewpoint is evident as it explicitly discusses the "objective of Inner Leadership" through the following declaration: "The fundamental question of 'How can

---

[33] Cf. Nicolas Holz, *Zurück in die Zukunft: Empfehlungen zur Wiederentdeckung und Weiterentwicklung der Inneren Führung* (BoD–Books on Demand, 2021), Annex 1/1 to 1/3 pp.128ff.
[34] Cf. op.Holz. pp. 15f.
[35] Cf op Holz. pp.32 and. 51.
[36] op. cit. Holz. p. 43f.

one serve well?' consequently fosters the development of a novel 'master narrative' of Inner Leadership."[37]

However, it is crucial to highlight that this approach must not create the impression of constantly chasing after every trend in order to cultivate the image of being "skilled" for the upcoming era. The notion of Inner Leadership ought not to be subjected to the perceived strain of adaptation.[38]

The initial premise should exhibit originality and lay a strong groundwork for subsequent arguments, thereby suggesting its potential *enduring relevance*.

Inner Leadership encompasses certain misconceptions, alongside the conventional notions of the "citizen in uniform" and "the spiritual armament." that are also used by Holz. One illustrative example that can be referenced is the adjective "*contemporary*", which is commonly utilized in various contexts. "Contemporary" presents significant difficulties due to its inherent *imprecision* and *variable* characteristics. The classification of contemporary individuals within a specific group residing in a particular region is inherently ambiguous due to the absence of consensus and the diverse nature of these groups, which are scattered throughout the republic. The variability is compromised by its inherent limitation of possessing a pre-established termination point. The significance of this matter is heightened within the framework of "contemporary leadership", given the diversity of linguistic norms and communication strategies across various regions. Consequently, certain language selections may be deemed unsuitable in different contexts. Moreover, if a linguistic and stylistic standard were to be universally embraced throughout Germany, it prompts inquiry into its longevity and legitimacy. Should a regulation governing individuals no longer be followed after ten years, based on the argument that it defines *itself* as contemporary and therefore includes a built-in temporal limitation within its definition? As a result, there are persuasive rationales for the existence of exclusively a "timeless democratic Inner Leadership" and "a militaristic leadership." The claim of being able to fully comprehend modern issues should be met with

---

[37] op. cit. Holz explicitly agrees with the essay by Sven Lange, who has already called for exactly this in 2020. Cf. Lange, „Fit für das 21. Jahrhundert: Warum die Konzeption der Inneren Führung eine neue Meistererzählung benötigt", pp.31ff.

[38] Cf. Holz, *Zurück in die Zukunft: Empfehlungen zur Wiederentdeckung und Weiterentwicklung der Inneren Führung*, pp.52ff.

skepticism, as individuals who hold this belief are surpassing their cognitive limitations.[39]

Another notable contribution that highlights the intention to strengthen the traditional concept of Inner Leadership is the publication of Helmut Jermer's book " Innere Führung kompakt. Eine Zusammenschau als Lehr- und Lernhilfsmittel." ("Inner Leadership compact. A synopsis as a teaching and learning tool.") in 2019. The author fulfills the commitments stated in his book, as he demonstrates a genuine interest in comprehending and assimilating the principles of Inner Leadership, as well as actively applying them in one's life.[40] The consistent incorporation of theological themes and literary references by Jermer serves to emphasize a pivotal aspect, while circumventing a purely scientific methodology.[41] Jermer effortlessly establishes an internal connection between the principles of Inner Leadership and the concept of human nature in the Basic Law, primarily due to the profound emotional attachment resulting from his Christian upbringing. The connection also encompasses contemplative elements that are observable in the printed prayers.[42] Jermer's assertion references a coherent storyline, particularly one that contains implicit Christian themes. The approach mentioned above is considered appropriate and valid, although it lacks universal applicability, which diverges from the author's intentions to advocate for tolerance, even in its current form. Jermer exhibits a notable degree of intellectual aptitude and consistently integrates the *notion of human conscience* into his elucidations. This concept is widely attributed to individuals and carries substantial importance within the ethical frameworks of diverse global religions.

---

[39] Konrad Liessmann, a philosopher from Vienna, is currently engaged in an investigation pertaining to the essence of contemporaneity (2022). The author explores the matter of differentiating between current and anachronistic aspects as a dialectical interaction including conformity to prevalent norms and divergence from them. The anachronistic aspect of every recall presents a challenge, as previous events are retrospectively evaluated through the lens of modern norms and criteria. The concepts presented by Liessmann possess notable pertinence, particularly with regards to the conservation of tradition within the Bundeswehr. The possible adverse consequences of applying modern evaluation standards to historical events can significantly compromise the integrity of historical study. The inclusion of Nietzsche in the argument is significant, since it implies that those who are untimely are not only nostalgic, but rather contemporaries who possess skepticism towards their own time period. In alignment with the scholarly contributions of Liessmann: In den Tiefen und auf den Höhen der Zeit. Konrad Paul Liessmann, „In der Tiefe und auf der Höhe der Zeit", *Neue Züricher Zeitung*, 9. April 2022.

[40] Helmut Jermer, *Innere Führung kompakt. Eine Zusammenschau als Lehr- und Lernhilfe.* (Berlin: Miles-Verlag, 2019), p.7.

[41] Christian motivation permeates the entire book. This is especially evident in chap. 3, "Committed to Peace." Cf. Jermer. pp. 65-71. In addition to prayers and quotations from Scripture, Jermer also invokes the encyclical "Gaudium et spes." Cf. Jermer.p. 85.

[42] Cf. op. cit. Jermer, *Innere Führung kompakt. Eine Zusammenschau als Lehr- und Lernhilfe*, p.120.

The sentence of utmost importance can be stated as follows: "As soldiers in the Bundeswehr, we serve in *conscientious obedience*. In order to stand before our conscience, we only obey what we can morally justify. 'Blind obedience' is out! In certain delicate situations, 'obedience' can mutate into personal cowardice. [43]"

This quotation not only expresses the concept of "conscientious obedience" in a noteworthy manner, but also makes a subtle reference to the historical backdrop of World War II. It offers guidance to the soldiers of the Bundeswehr, urging them to consider the actions of the soldiers who served in the Wehrmacht. It is recommended to consider adopting an alternative perspective in contrast to that put forth by the author. The lack of compatibility between the Wehrmacht and the traditions of the Bundeswehr was highlighted by the 2019 published Tradition Decree by the German Ministry of Defense. Situated within the Bundeswehr Command and Staff College in Hamburg, in close proximity to the dining hall, there exists a prominent visual representation that draws attention to the exemption of the German Armed Forces from the regrettable historical heritage associated with the Wehrmacht. The implementation of the Tradition Decree is credited with the establishment of this exemption. However, Jermer does not pass down this tradition to us. Despite the recent publication of his book, the author's ability to establish himself as a visionary remains unattained. Moreover, it is worth mentioning that the present proportion of Germans who maintain a religious affiliation amounts to approximately 50%.[44] The ongoing debate revolves around the extent to which soldiers born after 1990, who have grown up in a democratic society where democracy is considered a fundamental aspect of their lives, can effectively comprehend Inner Leadership through the lens of the negative tradition of the Wehrmacht. This is of particular relevance given the assertive manner in which Jermer presents this concept.

The third and final book being examined is "Innere Führung - Erfolge und Defizite der Führungsphilosophie für die Bundeswehr" (Inner Leadership - Achievements and Limitations of the Leadership Philosophy for the German Armed Forces), which was published in 2007. The work of Uwe Hartmann presents a collection of compelling sources obtained from social

---

[43] op. cit. Jermer. p. 66.
[44] Within specific portions of H. Jermer's publication, a distinct concept emerges, suggesting that Inner Leadership serves as an integral component of military chaplaincy. However, it is important to note that the actual relationship between the two is precisely the opposite. The perception emerges as a result of a lack of clarity surrounding persons who, by virtue of their guarded or unfavorable attitude towards the Catholic Church, also refuse to accept the notion of Inner Leadership. The original goal of the author may not be congruent with the present condition of the Catholic Church; yet, this can be observed.

discourse, accompanied by a dynamic exposition of the principles that underlie Inner Leadership. The consolidation process is the subject of this debate. The book, on the other hand, covers a wide range of themes. The book expertly demonstrates a significant level of thoroughness and vigour in information collecting and evaluation. The existing framework is deeply grounded in the compulsory military service of the Bundeswehr[45], highlighting the potential for interconnectivity between the Bundeswehr and society. The cessation of this specific service has led to an increased degree of societal apathy towards the Bundeswehr.[46]

Hartmann's exploration of Clausewitz's ideas holds significance within the conceptual framework of Inner Leadership in the field of systematics: "The dialectical relationship between peace and war, between democracy and the military, between freedom and obedience cannot be resolved with universally valid laws. There is no synthesis that could give absolute security to the politician and the soldier. Thus, the individual and his education, especially his strength of character, take on an outstanding importance for successful action. Education here means, in the sense of Scharnhorst and Clausewitz, the ability to find measures for action within oneself and to implement them resolutely.[47]"

The incorporation of this extensive quotation within the chapter entitled "Inner Leadership is a pragmatic concept" is suitable as it corresponds to the fundamental concept under examination. The presence of a diligent military personnel and their education, which correspond to the idea of aesthetic education as posited by Schiller[48], can be observed within the structure of Inner Leadership. A thorough comprehension of systematics requires a recognition and understanding of dialectics, as advocated by Hegel. Hartmann underscores the importance of a scholarly justification within the field of humanities, as he draws attention to the widely held belief in the Bundeswehr that "a sound theoretical framework represents the pinnacle of practicality. [49]"

According to Hartmann, it is argued that the process of fully comprehending Inner Leadership cannot be effectively summarized in a brief statement. It is crucial to acknowledge that the content presented thus far, as well as the forthcoming information, diverges significantly from the conventional reading material accessible to soldiers, thereby representing a notable departure

---

[45] Conscription to basic military service was suspended in March 2011 by the German Bundestag amending the German Conscription Act.
[46] Cf. Hartmann, *Innere Führung. Erfolge und Defizite der Führungsphilosophie für die Bundeswehr*, pp.134-143.
[47] Op. cit. Hartmann,.p. 75.
[48] Op. cit. Hartmann, p. 73.
[49] Op. cit. Hartmann, p. 73.

from the established norm. Nevertheless, if one were to argue that the preceding notion of Inner Leadership lacks a coherent framework, it becomes imperative to conduct a more thorough analysis and offer comprehensive justifications. Hartmann argues that "the concept of Inner Leadership possesses inherent complexity. To fully grasp the complexities of warfare, military operations, and the diverse array of challenges encountered by politics, society, and the Bundeswehr, it is essential to embrace a certain degree of complexity. There is a pressing requirement for the formulation of a theoretical framework pertaining to Inner Leadership, with the aim of efficiently structuring its complex characteristics, augmenting understanding, and bolstering the applicability of its underlying principles.[50]"

One can say that, in contemporary times, there has been a noticeable rise in the development of conceptual frameworks. Nicolas Holz utilizes a combination of textual analysis and visual representations in his scholarly endeavours to stimulate critical examination of the effectiveness of leadership. The investigation into the methods employed to achieve a task carries considerable significance, as it provides a more nuanced perspective in contrast to the straightforward question: "What precise actions are necessary to attain success?", which lacks a conclusive response. Helmut Jermer also employs conceptual analysis, highlighting the ethical framework that underlies the Christian viewpoint on human nature. This perspective can be regarded as a conceptual framework as it delineates the underlying principles of leadership by exploring the inquiries of "How and Why?" The limitations of this viewpoint, specifically in relation to its absence of universality, have already been expounded upon. Moreover, a relevant question emerges concerning the viability of incorporating the ethical principles found in the New Testament, as demonstrated by teachings like the Sermon on the Mount and similar passages, into the framework of military combat operations. Uwe Hartmann's scholarly contribution centers on his emphasis on the dialogical comprehension of education, as expounded. It is worth noting that other classical authors, including Wilhelm von Humboldt[51], could have also been included in this discussion.

---

[50] Op. cit. Hartmann, p. 216
[51] Cf. Wilhelm von Humboldt, *Wilhelm von Humboldt - Werke in fünf Bänden. Band I: Schriften zur Anthropologie und Geschichte*, hg. von 3 (Andreas Flitner und Klaus Giel, 1980), pp. 64, 71f, 236f.

2.1.2 Can the Basic Law be considered a reference point for Inner Leadership?

Individuals who strive to establish a rationale must identify a foundational premise that possesses inherent justifiability and does not necessitate additional justification. The book extensively examines a central theme that can be considered as a manifestation of common knowledge. A persistent question remains: What is the reasoning and democratic justification for participating in an independent discussion on the rationale and legitimization of Inner Leadership? Is it not enough to cite the German Basic Law as is commonly observed in the context of Inner Leadership?[52] The response to this inquiry will contribute as an additional fundamental element towards the establishment of the Inner Leadership axioms. Concurrently, in the realm of a critique, there emerges an inquiry concerning the fundamental principles upon which Inner Leadership can be based. They do not stem from the Basic Law. The clarification of this issue will be sought from Ernst Wolfgang Böckenförde (1930-2019), a prominent legal philosopher and former judge of the Federal Constitutional Court, as well as Hans Küng (1928-2021), a respected ethicist.

A functional liberal democratic state requires prerequisites that rely on each person's potential for understanding and that the state alone cannot provide. In the absence of this particular understanding, the efficacy of the Basic Law in offering support is diminished. This discussion centers on the Böckenförde dictum: "Thus the question of the binding forces arises anew and in its very essence: The *liberal, secularized state lives on preconditions that it cannot guarantee itself.* This is the great risk it has taken for the sake of freedom. On the one hand, it can exist as a liberal state only if the freedom it grants its citizens regulates itself from within, from the moral substance of the individual and the homogeneity of society. On the other hand, it cannot seek to guarantee these internal regulatory forces of its own accord, that is, by means of legal coercion and authoritative command, without giving up its freedom.[53]" According to the early Böckenförde, the presence of Catholicism is considered a necessary condition for the state to achieve a liberal nature. Böckenförde espouses support for this specific religious denomination, positing that it functions as a protective measure for the indispensable moral rectitude, while concurrently fostering cohesion within the ecclesiastical community. The legal philosopher alludes to the era of the German Empire until 1803, wherein the notion of Christian self-evidence conferred importance and intentionality upon the state, while also bestowing mercy upon its ruler. This sentiment, which is still

---

[52] Cf. C.-G. v Ilsemann, *Die Bundeswehr in der Demokratie. Zeit der Inneren* (Hamburg: Decker's Verlag, 1971).

[53] Ernst-Wolfgang Böckenförde, *Recht, Staat, Freiheit* (Frankfurt/Main, 1991), pp.112f..

common among people who identify as Christians, cannot be granted by the state alone. The above specified requirements are essential for the creation of a state, although they are not certain to be met.

The formulation of Böckenförde's viewpoint has played a pivotal role in shaping the path towards the axioms of Inner Leadership. embodies the *transformative* essence of faith. In 1987, Böckenförde further developed the fundamental notions of *moral substance and homogeneity*, reinterpreting them within the framework of a *democratic ethos*.[54] The author demonstrates an understanding of individuals who willingly take on the duty of preserving the notion of order and the ideals of democracy, transforming them into concrete behaviors.[55] This is not driven by obligation, but rather by personal volition. Böckenförde posits that the societal consensus pertaining to Catholicism experiences a metamorphosis into a democratic ethos.

When examining this argumentation from a scholarly standpoint, it is feasible to rephrase the Böckenförde dictum in a manner that can be effectively applied to the Inner Leadership of the Bundeswehr, while retaining its fundamental importance. *The efficacy of the free and democratic forces is contingent upon certain preconditions that it lacks the capacity to guarantee autonomously.* The establishment of a military's ethos and principles relies on the inherent autonomy of its personnel and cannot be exclusively governed by legislative measures. Likewise, society manifests a propensity for the presence of armed forces through its active engagement in the recruitment and deployment of both military personnel and civilian personnel. The notion of Inner Leadership promotes and encourages the voluntary adoption of democratic principles, thus facilitating the formation and maintenance of a democratic armed force.

In the year 1992, Böckenförde expounded: "Legal norms must be *able to* be followed out of insight.[56]" This formulation is notable from an ethical perspective as it places considerable emphasis on the notion of "ability". This viewpoint does not require unanimous consensus, but rather demands a presentation that is equally comprehensible to all individuals.[57] The present formulation does not solely pertain to a semantic discussion, but rather

---

[54] Ernst-Wolfgang Böckenförde, „Demokratie als Verfassungsprinzip", *Staat, Gesellschaft, Freiheit: Studien zur Staatstheorie und zum Verfassungsrecht*, 1992, pp.359ff..

[55] Cf. Anna Katharina Mangold, „Das Böckenförde-Diktum", Mai 2019, https://verfassungsblog.de/das-boeckenfoerde-diktum/.Mangold A.K.: Das Böckenförde-Diktum, p. 5.

[56] quoted from Mangold A.K.: Das Böckenförde-Diktum. p. 6.

[57] It is important to acknowledge that Böckenförde's formulation aligns closely with Immanuel Kant's ethical framework, as outlined in his work "Grundlegung zur Metaphysik der Sitten" (GMS). There exist a comprehensive set of seven formulations for the categorical imperative. There are five instances in which the term "can/können" is present. According to Kant, the act of committing oneself in freedom entails that the need of one's actions can be universally recognized.

represents a substantial expression that harmonizes two intricate notions, specifically universality and freedom. Universally valid propositions refer to statements that are formulated and intended in a manner that *enables* individuals of good will to perceive and accept them.

Hans Küng, the renowned Swiss theologian and ethicist, presents a perspective that closely aligns with the aforementioned viewpoint.

Following his dispute with the Vatican, he embarked on the development of the "Global Ethic Project"[58], mirroring a trajectory akin to Böckenförde's transition from the theological realm to the ethical domain. "In accordance with its constitution, the democratic state must respect, protect and promote freedom of conscience and religion, as well as all other modern human rights, and promote them. And yet, in all this, the state may not decree a sense of life and a lifestyle, it may not legally prescribe supreme values and ultimate norms if it does not want to violate its ideological neutrality. - This is quite obviously the dilemma of every modern democratic state (...): What it may not legally prescribe, it is at the same time dependent on.[59]" This phenomenon has significant implications at the state level, encompassing the Inner Leadership of the Bundeswehr. Setting specific values is not permitted. The assertion that 'It is good and right if ...' exhibits a lack of universal applicability and cannot be further expounded upon in a manner that possesses universal binding authority. Therefore, one could contend that the inclusion of Inner Leadership in the framework is intrinsically flawed, as its content faces inherent limitations and is bound to confront them unavoidably. Ultimately, this is why a regulation on Inner Leadership is also invalid, because it quickly reaches and must reach its limits in terms of content. This automatically makes it difficult and impossible to say *what* Inner leadership is. This issue is further intensified by the fact that, despite the doctrine inherent implausibility, it would require formalization as a regulation in order to establish a persuasive authority within the military. Is it possible to argue that the essential elements required to create a cohesive community—which, in the end, leads to the successful completion of a mission—cannot be imposed upon or prescribed?

The ability to determine the *material nature* is unachievable, but it is possible to determine its *modal* or *formal* characteristics. This form of determination relates to the manner or prescribed methodology by which something ought to be done and identifies the specific areas of activity associated with it. In the classical sense, the role of "Critique" entails the assessment and examination of a particular subject matter. Hence, it is imperative that *all axioms concerning Inner Leadership are formulated with respect to the mode. This analysis offers a*

---

[58] Cf. Hans Küng, *Projekt Weltethos* (München: Piper, 1990), pp. 46-57.
[59] Op. cit. Küng. p. 49.

comprehensive examination of the potential practical uses of Inner Leadership, while refraining from imposing specific guidelines or recommendations.

Therefore, the primary emphasis of the military sphere of influence is exclusively centered on issues related to spirit, attitude, and responsibility. It is possible to argue that Inner Leadership represents the fundamental spiritual nature of the armed forces, explaining the moral principles and prevailing social culture that the armed forces are inspired by and get their identity from. It gets visible whether the superior's priority is love of humanity and freedom or small-mindedness and narrow-minded fearfulness in order to revert the subordinate to the status of a subject, which the undemocratic superior himself essentially is due to a lack of courage and esprit. Only those who actively promote and support the sentiment of humanity and the principle of liberty are eager to safeguard this civilization, even if it means jeopardizing their own lives and physical well-being. Therefore, Inner Leadership is the driving force behind the desire to defend (dt.:"Wehrwille").[60]

Someone who has reached spiritual emancipation is able to understand the significance of laws and is obligated to follow them. This argument is based on the idea that all rules and values that exist within a certain society are inherently legitimate. These things have worth because people in the society have purposefully assigned it to them, not because of how they were created or forced to exist. Thus, it is possible to argue that, within a particular culture, a pluralistic society could be seen as ideal. It is reasonable to think that an individual, bound by a formal affirmation or an employment contract to the government, may support the importance of a diverse and multi-perspective society. However, it is not feasible to ensure that he is *speaking* with sincerity, that he truly *understands* the meaning of what he is saying, that he is willing to accept them, and that he is ready to defend them as a soldier, all while putting his life and physical health in danger and putting his family at risk as a result of this choice. However, this particular understanding can be shared, observed, internalized, and fully accepted.

---

[60] Therefore, these explanations already take into account the fifth axiom. The distinction between discussing the affection towards humanity and the affection towards liberty, as opposed to discussing the desire for liberty and the regard for humanity, carries significance. Please refer to Chapter 4.5 for further details.

2.2 Axioms in Rhetoric and Communication Studies

The notion of *axioms* has previously been introduced and defined as fundamental principles that *do not require justification*. Additional clarification is necessary to elucidate this.

The concept of axioms can be traced back to the rhetorical theories of Blaise Pascal (1623-1662), particularly as expounded in his work "The Art of Persuasion" (L'Art de persuader, 1660). At the outset, there was a mere anticipation regarding the potential significance of this concept within the framework of a novel narrative of Inner Leadership, as no established theory or system was in place at that juncture. The persistent efforts to formulate a comprehensive definition of Inner Leadership serve as a compelling exemplification. However, individuals who are seeking a systematic approach necessitate a fundamental basis that is autonomous and not derived from any external origin, commonly referred to as axioms.

This term exhibits two distinct advantages. The notion of *Inner Leadership* encompasses a novel concept, and the lack of preconceived ideas greatly facilitates the creation of a new narrative. Moreover, the term exhibits a noteworthy attribute of being easily remembered because of the inherent brilliance connected to the term 'axiom'.

The field of rhetoric primarily focuses on the skillful use of language to persuade and enhance understanding among individuals. Concurrently, it is crucial to take into account the ethical maturation of the orator, given the historical differentiation between the practices of persuasion and conviction. The application of persuasive techniques encompasses a broad spectrum of objectives, and it is not possible to ascertain the true intention behind a speech without further examination.

This phenomenon is now known as the instrumentalization of language. In contrast, convincing entails the process of identifying and clarifying verifiable truths, often communicated with benevolent intentions. Pascal's main area of interest lies in the domain of convincing, where achieving success requires the establishment of axioms that can be universally acknowledged as true by all members of the audience. There are established guidelines pertaining to this specific matter:

"*Rules for axioms.* - 1. not to admit any necessary principle, however clear and evident it may be, without having ascertained whether one accepts it. 2. a*dmit as axioms only what is perfectly evident in itself.*[61]"

Pascal's concept is derived from the idea that when axioms are self-evident and straightforward, the need to inquire about their universal acceptance

---

[61] Blaise Pascal, *Die Kunst zu Überzeugen* (Heidelberg: Lambert Schneider, 1963). p.93.

becomes superfluous. Hence, significant importance is attributed to the *perfect evidence* cited in the second point. [62] Nevertheless, it is important to acknowledge that within Pascal's specific context, the concept of "acceptance" holds considerable significance, as it corresponds to the ideas of overall validity and the *ability* to willingly embrace and understand, as previously expounded upon by Böckenförde, Küng, and Kant.

Point 2: Establishing evidence, that is, making it obvious to everybody, presents challenges. This discourse consistently explores the dynamic relationship between truth, probability, and the construction of reality. Nevertheless, the existence of societal heterogeneity presents difficulties in producing impeccable evidence. Fortunately, it is not imperative to argue that evidence must be convincing to every individual, as the primary goal of evidence should be to achieve *internal consistency* and coherence. As a result, the person receiving the information is not seen as the whole total of their prior experiences and knowledge. Rather, they are regarded as a cognitive being that can separate from their own personal perspective and actively interact verbally with a notion in an impartial and sensitive way. This statement can be interpreted as an expression of Hegel's perspective on education, in which he sees it as a mechanism through which the spirit achieves a sense of detachment from itself[63] by actively and systematically scrutinizing concepts while consistently avoiding the tendency to position oneself as the ultimate criterion or frame of reference for comprehension. During the cognitive process and the acquisition of knowledge, individuals are required to possess the capacity to detach themselves from their personal biases and perspectives. This detachment is necessary in order to engage in a critical evaluation of the validity of a *thought or idea*. It's another matter entirely whether or not the author consistently sticks to this concept, what personal meaning it holds, or whether or not the outcome is appreciated.

Nevertheless, it is noteworthy to acknowledge the existing tension between the concepts of truth and probability.[64] The discipline of rhetoric finds themself in a state of contention with the concept of truth, as the understanding of truth within metaphysical philosophy is consistently linked to the idea of

---

62 Axioms of Inner Leadership are also named by Sven Lange. (Lange, „Fit für das 21. Jahrhundert: Warum die Konzeption der Inneren Führung eine neue Meistererzählung benötigt", pp.36ff). However, he does not explain the rhetorical term, but relates it historically to the beginnings of Inner Leadership.

63 Georg Wilhelm Friedrich Hegel, *Phänomenologie des Geistes* (Hamburg: Wessels, H.-F. und Clairmont, H. Meiner, 1988), pp. 64, 71f, 236f..

64 For those who would like to go into this in more detail, the book by Giambattista Vico "Liber metaphysicus" (1710) recommended. Also by the same author: De nostri temporis studiorum ratione. (1708) Lat./Dt.

certainty, as denoted by the Latin term "certum." However, it can be argued that what can be deemed certain is solely derived from the conceptual framework, without being influenced by any empirical observations. One illustrative example relates to the observation that the magnitude of a component is consistently smaller when compared to the whole. While this *geometric statement* may be deemed trustworthy, its informational significance is constrained. However, in the case of phenomena that necessitate visual observation, the achievement of absolute truth becomes unachievable. Therefore, it is incumbent upon the speaker to present a fact in *the most plausible or veracious manner feasible.*

Individuals who argue against the necessity of this philosophical distinction may find it beneficial to reflect upon the wide range of individuals encountered within the military offices. The geometric character ("It's true because it's true"), distinguished by its precise delineation and inherent clarity, encompasses an understanding of the fundamental principles that pertain to its being. The individual under consideration exhibits a predilection for utilizing numerical data, lists, and Excel tables as the principal sources of importance. The individual demonstrates a comprehensive understanding of empirical knowledge, which establishes the parameters within which they navigate. He approaches any additional information with a skeptical mindset. The portrayal of this geometric soldier in its pure form poses a significant obstacle to the notion of Inner Leadership. During pivotal moments, it may not always be practical to encapsulate the intricacies of existence within the boundaries of an Excel spreadsheet. The persistent issue of evaluators in positions of authority exhibiting one-sidedness poses significant challenges.

The contemporary scholar who engages in the examination of axioms within non-mathematical domains frequently references Paul Watzlawick (1921-2007), an Austrian communication scientist.[65] Although it may be considered a slight deviation from the central theme of Inner Leadership, this digression possesses significance for two separate reasons: First and foremost, it is important to acknowledge that the communicative axioms put forth by Watzlawick have potential applicability to the leaders within the armed forces, as they consistently employ communication as a fundamental tool for exercising leadership. The concept of pure factual information is not present in any form of communication, as all modes of expression contain additional dimensions beyond the mere conveyance of facts. Moreover, it is apparent that Watzlawick's approach has been employed in the development of the axioms of Inner Leadership. Watzlawick consistently adheres to a structured

---

[65] Cf. Paul Watzlawick. und Janet H. Beavin. Don D. Jackson, *Menschliche Kommunikation. Formen – Störungen – Paradoxien*, Bd. 11 (Bern: Verlag Hans Huber, 2007), pp.50-71.

approach in his work, wherein he introduces his axioms at the outset, proceeds to offer further elaboration, and subsequently supports them with empirical evidence. However, it is important to note that a significant differentiation can be observed: This book relies on carefully selected references to the literature of Inner Leadership instead of using empirical evidence, in order to support and validate the coherence of its content.[66]

Watzlawick's first axiom of communication asserts that it is inherently *impossible to not communicate*. In the realm of scholarly discourse surrounding Watzlawick, it is common to come across the recurring statement that the notion of being unable to *not* communicate constitutes a fundamental concept within communication theory. The domain of communication encompasses not only spoken language, but also diverse paralinguistic phenomena including vocal intonation, speech tempo, pauses, laughter, and sighing. Moreover, nonverbal cues, encompassing body language and a range of behaviors, including silence, exert a substantial influence on the process of communication. The phenomenon of physical absence can also function as a mode of communication. Numerous modalities of communication possess the ability to exert an impact on individuals, prompting them to react in either deliberate or inadvertent manners. Since everyone always acts and reacts at the same moment, we may therefore conclude that even if we have logical pre- and post-timelines in our self-behavior (A reacts to B), in reality we have a simultaneity of multiple types of communication that are difficult to discern in cause and effect. Additional to the findings of Watzlawick, metalingual communication is observed to take place, primarily through non-verbal means such as gestures and facial expressions. This form of communication, which surpasses verbal expression, has been observed to evoke responses from individuals from the early stages of their life.

Watzlawick's second axiom of communication asserts that each instance of *communication encompasses both the content and relationship dimensions*. In relation to the content, the initial accuracy of the information holds no significance. Moreover, it is crucial to take into account the sender's intended understanding of the content by the recipient as an equally important aspect. This axiom is frequently prone to misinterpretation, especially when it comes to the receiver's understanding of the sender's intended message. Considering the inherent variability in individual interpretations, it is observed that such misinterpretations often correspond to a constructivist viewpoint. Nevertheless,

---

[66] There is potential for establishing connections between the axioms of communication and those of Inner Leadership. However, for the sake of enhancing comprehension, this task will not be undertaken in this context. The examination of this subject matter would warrant a separate topic of discussion.

the central aspect under consideration pertains to the individual initiating the action and their intention, rather than the individual receiving it, who may be fully awake or in a state of partial wakefulness and may experience different levels of consciousness. The individual who initiates communication bears the responsibility of articulating the nature of the relationship. The final determination regarding the content that a receiver chooses to transmit in response lies within their own discretion. One crucial factor to consider is that in cases of effective and natural communication, the relational aspect tends to diminish in importance because of the shared comprehension of intentions. In instances of communication marked by conflict, it is crucial to carefully revise both the content and form of each message. It is imperative to underscore the primacy of the relationship over the level of information, as the latter solely pertains to facts. Hierarchically, the *manner* in which this is dealt with assumes a superior position. Watzlawick offers a mathematical elucidation for this phenomenon. The constituents present in the dataset can be comprehended as numerical quantities, whereas their associations bear resemblance to the mathematical construct known as a correlation coefficient. The significance and meaning of numerical values are acquired through interrelationships. Metacommunication encompasses all forms of communication, as the underlying message being conveyed extends beyond the explicit content.

Watzlawick's third axiom of communication asserts that events are punctuated in a sequential manner, suggesting that communication is inherently characterized by *cause-and-effect relationships*. The initial axiom postulated that communication exhibits both a logical and a tangible sequence. The third presupposes the first. What supplementary details are provided? Initially, it is important to note that cultural customs are widely recognized as socially acceptable and suitable within a given nation, aligning with a distinct set of norms and values. Punctuation is therefore a sequence. The concept is exemplified by the commonly observed occurrence in which decisions were historically made with reduced necessity for explanation and justification. Within the realm of communication science, it is evident that *punctuation* has experienced alterations that are shaped by cultural influences. However, the usage of punctuation is type-specific. Watzlawick proposes a differentiation between individuals who assume positions of leadership and those who are followers. Each mode of communication possesses the capacity to develop into a habitual behavior, suggesting that it is influenced by causal relationships. Nevertheless, it is important to note that this particular process does not take place within the immediate context of the sender and receiver. Instead, it unfolds gradually over an extended period, thereby facilitating the formation and cultivation of a *habitus*. The axiom in question holds considerable importance for the field of Inner Leadership, as it provides a solution to the persistent question regarding the feasibility of implementing Inner Leadership in combat situations. Individuals who have developed a habit of assuming leadership positions based on the principles of Inner Leadership cultivate a personal disposition that embodies the characteristics of a leader. This disposition inherently includes adopting a democratic approach to the profession of a soldier. The provision of service by an individual is shaped by the character that is cultivated during the course of this undertaking. Consequently, this dynamic has an impact on their professional and interpersonal behavior towards their subordinates, whom the superior supports and who collaboratively contribute to the achievement of their shared objectives. This certainty can also be applicable in the case of an extreme. It is advisable to clearly articulate this mindset and embody it as a guiding principle, thereby serving as a manifestation of one's individual conscience.[67]

The fourth axiom of communication asserts that *human communication encompasses both analogue and digital modalities.* The use of terminology in this particular context bears resemblance to outdated technological concepts, wherein the importance of electric tubes and transistors in *digital* computers persists. This observation serves to emphasize the notion that the origins of psychology and communication theory can be attributed to the natural sciences rather than the humanities. The potential presence of multiple occurrences of analogous behavior within the same digital nomenclature holds considerable importance. What may initially appear to be intricate can ultimately be comprehended as uncomplicated. The concept of "silence" within the digital realm has the potential to obfuscate various analogue actions. Silence can serve as a method of conveying agreement ("Yes, you're right."), resignation ("Whether I say something or not, remains the same."), horror-induced paralysis ("I'm so shocked that I don't know what to say."), strategic calculation ("I'll say something about it later and think about it still."), or as an expression of nefarious intentions ("If I don't say anything, when the boss comes, it makes him fall apart even more."). The widely accepted maxim of "*qui tacet, consentiret*" or "he who is silent agrees" does not universally adhere to its application. The notion of "crying" encompasses a range of emotional manifestations, such as joy, sorrow, pain, compassion, and calculation. Likewise, the term "laughter" can be interpreted as a reaction to various stimuli such as humor, tickling, feelings of shame, insecurity, adaptive behavior, intentional actions, or deceitful intentions. Furthermore, the act of "verbal communication" serves a multitude of functions, including the transmission of information, the manifestation of personal identity, the expression of vulnerability, the avoidance of substantive

---

[67] Cf. Hannes Wendroth, *Gute Führung - (k)ein Selbstgänger. Kleine Führungshilfe mit praktischen Hinweisen und persönlichen Anmerkungen.* (Berlin: Miles-Verlag, 2022), pp. 18ff.

discourse, and the demonstration of courtesy. The digital component primarily relates to the object, whereas the analogue component relates to the relationship.[68] Nevertheless, it is important to acknowledge that analogue actions exhibit a degree of digital indeterminacy. Watzlawick offers an elucidation for this phenomenon through the utilization of a metaphor involving a tightly closed hand. This phenomenon can encompass both proclivities towards aggression as well as the capacity for self-control. Ambiguity is an inherent characteristic of every action, as digital designations have the capacity to generate multiple actions. The comprehension of this concept enriches an individual's viewpoint and cognitive capacities, ultimately drawing inspiration from Heraclitus' original quotation. Heraclitus posits that the soul is required to exercise discernment in its decision-making process, whereby it must judiciously choose suitable actions and motives from a wide array of possibilities, contingent upon the prevailing circumstances.

The fifth axiom of communication can be stated as follows: *Communication can be symmetrical or complementary.* Symmetrical behavior is observed in instances where two elements, characterized by a singular connection, undergo continuous development. The dynamic described above can be categorized in contemporary discourse as a type of partnership or companionate interaction that is characterized by mutual equality. In this type of interaction, both individuals work together towards achieving a higher state collectively. On the other hand, the notion of complementarity entails a hierarchical model of progression, in which one entity assumes a dominant position indicating *superiority*, while the other entity assumes a subordinate position indicating *inferiority*. Nevertheless, the absence of moral significance in this context suggests that it falls outside the realm of being classified as either "strong" or "weak," instead aligning more closely with a cultural framework. The hierarchical relationship between a superior and a subordinate is characterized by the dependence of the latter on the former. The primary position of the superior determines the secondary position of the subordinate, and vice versa. Each entity defines and orients itself in relation to the other.

---

[68] Silence poses a potential pitfall for military leaders, as it can serve as a deceptive cover for concealed intentions under a mask of compliance. The concept of maintaining a unique mode of communication through silence, which was erroneously interpreted as assent and loyalty to the detriment of his superiors, was previously explored by Jaroslav Hašek in his portrayal of the character Schweyk.

2.3 A New Narrative - A New Master Narrative - A New Inner Leadership

In the year 2020, Sven Lange, author of the essay "Fit für das 21. Jahrhundert" (Fit for the 21st century), put forth a proposal for the creation of a novel comprehensive framework pertaining to Inner Leadership. The essay being examined exhibits a historical nature, offering a succinct overview of the progression of Inner Leadership up to the current era, all within a restricted page count. Moreover, whether it is intentional or merely conveyed as an ancillary comment, the author presents a strongly conclusive indication of the potential attributes associated with a hypothetical concept known as Inner Leadership, while abstaining from delineating precise boundaries or limitations. The intention of this statement is not to create the Inner Leadership that Lange aspires to, but rather to establish a framework from which a new and unique Inner Leadership can be developed.

The discovery of the *Protestant roots of Inner Leadership* may be perceived as a somewhat surprising revelation, given the limited extent of Lange's discourse on the subject and the discreet placement of certain references in a footnote. "The critique frequently levied against Inner Leadership pertains to its purported focus on intellect and rationality, neglecting the role of emotions and spirituality. This criticism can be attributed to the Protestant-influenced orientation of Inner Leadership, which places significant emphasis on reason and duty as primary sources of motivation.[69]" - The act of engaging in introspective reflection and self-disclosure, commonly referred to as confessions, has become progressively unfamiliar to the majority of individuals in present-day society. Böckenförde posits that the advancement of thought necessitates surpassing the limitations imposed by Christianity, and instead embracing a mode of thinking referred to by Hans Küng as a "global ethic"[70]. Nevertheless, this claim is not valid for the approximate timeframe of 1950, during which the core principles of Inner Leadership, which continue to be applicable in the present day, were established in the Himmerode Memorandum.

It is worth noting that Inner Leadership demonstrates identifiable patterns of Protestant thought, particularly focused on the principle of '*sola scriptura*'. This principle highlights the exclusive authority of the written word and its resulting influence. This particular approach is founded upon a sense of obligation and places emphasis on the implementation of principles that can be *recorded in written format*. Attitude and a democratic outlook must be the

---

[69] Lange, „Fit für das 21. Jahrhundert: Warum die Konzeption der Inneren Führung eine neue Meistererzählung benötigt", p.39. Lange also refers to two essays by Angelika Dörfler-Dierken from 2005 and 2007, which focus on the Christian-Protestant roots of Inner Leadership.
[70] Küng, *Projekt Weltethos*.

decisive pillars of Inner Leadership, as rules and concrete descriptions always fall short and can lead to paradoxical prescriptions. In the course of this book, it became evident that cultivating a good attitude and adopting a democratic perspective are the essential elements of Inner Leadership. This problem originates from the limitations of depending only on prescriptive norms and exact explanations, which can create contradicting results. The perspective is strengthened by the setting of Inner Leadership, in which a strong emotional relationship to the public and a devotion to a nation founded on the principles of freedom and equality are key. The phenomenon of experiencing affection cannot be ascribed to cognitive processes; rather, it is a gift, or *gratia*. The central theme of Inner Leadership seems to center on the attainment of a deep comprehension of the notion of Inner Leadership as a gift.

The recognition of Inner Leadership as a gift is of particular importance when endeavoring to articulate it through *language* and convey it through complex sentence structures. For example: "Inner Leadership, under the impression of societal, security-political, and technological and further changes, is to be understood as a dynamic conception aimed at constant further development. (...).[71]". The determination of the future trajectory of Inner Leadership cannot be solely reliant on the process of adjusting it to different contextual elements, both real and hypothetical. The quotation exemplifies the absence of a concrete systematic for Inner Leadership. When faced with a concept that lacks semantic significance, the capacity to mentally represent it becomes unachievable, rendering it very incompatible with the notion of Inner Leadership.

The notion of Inner Leadership is clearly evident in the development of policies and regulations, suggesting a robust integration of this principle. The German doctrine on Inner Leadership demonstrates a clear manifestation of this phenomenon. The primary emphasis of the discourse is only on the constituent components of Inner Leadership. The significance of comprehension is often undervalued. The matter at hand pertains to the execution of the "commandments of rules of the Bundeswehr."

The fundamental concept of Inner Leadership, which centers around its alignment with the Basic Law, may be traced back to the Protestant past.[72] However, the task of identifying soldiers who are willing to connect their service

---

[71] Th Martin, „Innere Führung zwischen Zeitenwende und Megatrends", *Alumni FüAk online*, 26. September 2022.

[72] The focus on the intersection between law and ethics appears to have been predominantly pursued by Ulrich de Maizière. The entirety of his publication "Führen im Frieden" (1974) is founded upon this principle.

and conduct with the principles of Inner Leadership, in order to preserve the Basic Law, may provide a potential difficulty. The response to this inquiry is dependent on an individual's capacity for understanding and self-reflection in their day-to-day experiences. The objective of this study is to provide a comprehensive analysis of the practical application of Inner Leadership in a modern military institution, thereby giving substance to its theoretical underpinnings.

The matter of Inner Leadership, necessitating in-depth analysis, transcends the scope of the Basic Law, subordinate laws, and directives. This statement explores the deeper motivations behind the *pursuit* of democratic constitutionality. The origin of the Basic Law can be ascribed to the aforementioned intention and the belief in its legitimacy, as the law cannot be deduced from another legislation. Broadly speaking, a law can be comprehended as an obligatory provision. The imperative inside Germany is derived from a collective aspiration for both freedom and justice. The soldiers serving in the German armed services make a solemn commitment to courageously protect the principles of law and the freedoms of the German citizenry. Therefore, our propensity to participate in conflict also stems from this desire. Laws, especially the Basic Law, are subordinate to the fundamental ideals of freedom and justice. From a contemporary perspective, it is apparent that the will does not hold superiority over the law; instead, it logically and temporally precedes it.[73] One possible concern comes when the constitution no longer corresponds with the collective wishes and preferences of the population.

In the endeavor to develop the principles of Inner Leadership, it is crucial to recognize and give precedence to the fundamental values of democracy. These values play a vital role in stimulating and maintaining a sincere dedication to democracy, coming before the enactment of any fundamental laws. The axioms obtained from the systematics of Inner Leadership, which will be further elaborated upon, are clearly not to be interpreted as prescriptive laws and regulations. The establishment of *attitudes* is vital, originating from the fundamental principles of democracy. This has the potential to facilitate the establishment of democratic norms and, to a certain extent, enhance the level of rigor and enforceability inside the Bundeswehr. Nevertheless, it is imperative to recognize that the fundamental nature of Inner Leadership, which is unattainable through written texts, must perpetually remain elusive. The suggested methodology involves a restructuring of Inner Leadership, placing emphasis on the necessity of a significant divergence from a solely technical and geometric framework.

---

[73] Cf. Manfred Görtemaker, *Geschichte der Bundesrepublik Deutschland: von der Gründung bis zur Gegenwart* (München: C.H. Beck, 1999), pp. 44-82.

It is important to acknowledge, with great importance, that within the context of Inner Leadership, the commitment to the democratic narrative can inherently and seamlessly function as a guiding principle. Up until now, the justification for the pursuit of further development and reorientation, akin to the scenario observed in Lange's case, has continuously been based on the changed conditions surrounding the Bundeswehr. The consideration of various components such as operational reality, downsizing, hybrid risks, political and religious extremism, intercultural competencies, digitalization of command processes, diversity and variety, and the challenges of balancing family and career is crucial in the conceptualization process. The failure to promptly integrate these aspects not only presents a risk of rendering the conceptualization outdated, but also undermines the viability of the entire notion of Inner Leadership.[74] - The justification for the existence of a diverging perspective lies in the fact that the material aligned with Lange's assertions can be seen not as an all-encompassing notion, but rather as a unique depiction of a convolute that contains several aspects, leading to a state of complexity. The aforementioned Manual on Inner Leadership, which was developed between the years 2022 and 2023, serves as a notable illustration of this phenomenon, as suggested by preliminary research findings. The notion of Inner Leadership should be approached with prudence to prevent bearing the responsibility of being the Bundeswehr's sole repository for unsolved matters that cannot be adequately addressed by either the military or society.

---

[74] Cf. Lange, „Fit für das 21. Jahrhundert: Warum die Konzeption der Inneren Führung eine neue Meistererzählung benötigt", p.44.

3   Systematics of Inner Leadership

The notable level of interest exhibited by politicians and significant segments of the general population inside our nation towards Inner Leadership can be seen as a manifestation of their recognition and regard for the Bundeswehr. There is a widespread desire for a military force that is actively engaged, operational, and capable of fostering a sense of identification among individuals. In pursuit of this objective, civil society places certain requirements on the armed forces, which are appropriately grounded in a democratic self-perception. Those conditions primarily pertain to the internal framework, namely the *manner in which it operates*, and encompass *three fundamental inquiries* that serve as the foundation for Inner Leadership.

1. What are the preferred modes of collaboration within the armed forces?
2. What are the values that influence and direct the behavior of a soldier?
3. Ideally, what is the nature of the integration between the armed forces and society?

The German doctrine "Innere Führung Selbstverständnis und Führungskultur" (Inner Leadership Self-Image and Leadership Culture), which was last updated in 2008, has unquestionably played a significant role in this matter. The fundamental tenets of regulation have become deeply ingrained throughout the operations of the Bundeswehr to the extent that they are frequently overlooked as commonplace. As health is for a vital human and freedom is for an independent citizen, democratic cooperation in the Bundeswehr is a standard that is often taken for granted until errors or missteps arise. However, it is these particular errors that serve as indicators of the significance of Inner Leadership, rendering it an optimal and remedial undertaking with a clear purpose.

The doctrine under discussion holds significant importance, particularly due to its nearly 15-year existence, necessitating careful examination in light of the evolving global landscape, national context, and armed forces dynamics. The necessity of specific adjustments in this context must be demonstrated by a procedure that can identify the precise areas of concern and determine the appropriate measures for preservation. In the work of Marcel Bohnert (2017), there are indications that shed light on a longstanding tension that has been effectively addressed for several decades, specifically by Friedrich Schiller in 1795. Another significant aspect of Inner Leadership will be examined by G.W.F. Hegel (1801), with the intention of afterwards giving voice to the French philosopher Emmanuel Lévinas (1978).

3.1   Polarization as the beginning of the thought process

Marcel Bohnert (2017) explores the concept of opposites and addresses the inherent potential for conflict in his book on Inner Leadership. The prologue authored by Gerhard Brugmann, a former Major General of the German Army, provides evident visibility of this fact: "The soldier must cultivate characteristics for his deployment that put him at odds with his democratic state order, which is based on human rights [75]". The presence of contrasting elements is a prominent feature throughout the entirety of the book. Regrettably, Bohnert concludes his analysis of this unresolved dichotomy without offering any additional insights. Consequently, he subjects Inner Leadership to scrutiny, as implied by the book's title, albeit with a certain degree of reluctance towards endorsing it fully.

However, it is important to note that this particular aspect, which presents a fresh perspective within the discourse, does not necessarily need to materialize. The presence of a potential relationship among the three aforementioned philosophical authors is evident and warrants a further examination. Therefore, the significance of Inner Leadership can manifest in various circumstances throughout a soldier's life, as it offers the potential to reconcile this inherent duality. Inner Leadership has the capacity to address the inquiries posed by the "Generation Deployment," a group in which Bohnert identifies himself as a representative, provided that they are situated inside a framework that requires further development.

The polarity already alluded to is exemplified multiple times by Bohnert through the juxtaposition of *Sparta* and *Athens*.[76] The contrasting attitudes of the two entities may be observed in their approach towards *conflict and decision-making*. One entity adopts a more *aggressive and efficient stance*, while the other prioritizes a *civilian and deliberative process* that takes into account the state's democratic values, freedom, peace, and justice. In 2014, Bohnert highlighted the existing dichotomy between *military professionalism* (also professionalization in the trade) and *politization*.[77]

Regrettably, he persists in adhering to this state of irreconcilability and ultimately expresses a preference for professionalism over politicization. It is worth noting that the term politicization carries a negative connotation, as he

---

[75] Bohnert, *Innere Führung auf dem Prüfstand.* The author appears to lack awareness regarding the distinction between a contradiction and a correlation, as the observed phenomenon can be better understood as a correlation of effects. As demonstrated in the forthcoming analysis, Brugmann draws upon Ulrich de Maizière's concept of the "paradox" inherent in the soldier's occupation, which also entails a constrained and dichotomous perception of reality.

[76] Cf. op. cit. Bohnert. pp. 28, 149ff

[77] See also Richard Drexl und Josef Kraus, *Nicht einmal bedingt abwehrbereit. Die Bundeswehr zwischen Elitetruppe und Reformruine.* (München: FBVerlag, 2019).

suggests that "actual experience should serve as a corrective measure for theoretical frameworks (...).[78]" Nevertheless, such actions would result in severe repercussions, as evidenced by several instances that directly contradict the principles outlined in the Basic Law and Inner Leadership. This is due to the fact that prioritizing practical implementation would ultimately lead to adverse outcomes. The efficacy of the practice dictates our actions. Bohnert (2014) acknowledges the potential outcomes that may arise when a theoretical framework is derived from practical experiences, as exemplified by the existence of numerous informal rules and, notably, the "Ten Commandments of the Paratroopers".[79] Bohnert argues that both Inner Leadership *and* informal codes serve a purpose, with the former being relevant for administrative personnel and the latter for active soldiers. The presented thesis lacks viability in its current form and does not align with the principles of an inclusive and comprehensive leadership culture. The yet-to-be-defined axioms will demonstrate their applicability to all individuals inside the Bundeswehr. They exhibit a tendency to come together in situations when others discuss the concept of division.

A question arises as a consequence of prioritizing military drill and efficiency over critical thought, as evidenced in the period leading up to the First World War. Europe has witnessed the development of weapons that have shown to be effective in practical applications since the conclusion of the arms race within the Franco-German War in 1870/71. The perceived dominance in implementation observed in certain nations, such as Germany, has significantly contributed to the eventual dissemination and development of theoretical concepts. The prospect of a conflict as a means unto itself became increasingly imminent, and during the process of escalation, purported justifications were added in order to maintain a perception of moral purity. Individuals who prioritize practical application above theoretical understanding find themselves deviating from the correct path sooner than anticipated, and then have challenges in disentangling themselves from the consequences of their actions. The excessive emphasis on military technological capabilities also carries the significant risk of being politically and ideologically

---

[78] Bohnert, *Innere Führung auf dem Prüfstand*, p. 32. This aspect is noteworthy as Bohnert places particular emphasis in his comparative portfolio "Sparta vs. Athens" on the fundamental concept of the state, which ultimately led to its own demise. The decline of Sparta's prominence and power during the 4th century B.C. can be attributed, in part, to the stringent enforcement of the exclusivity of its warrior caste, known as hoplites, which ultimately led to its slow self-abolishment.

[79] op. cit. Sönke Neitzel, *Deutsche Krieger. Vom Kaiserreich zur Berliner Republik – eine Militärgeschichte* (Berlin: Ullstein, 2022), pp. 287-298.

exploited.[80] Uwe Hartmann skillfully emphasizes how important political wisdom is to the moral fibre of a devoted soldier in a democracy military. Nevertheless, the author also highlights the allure of establishing a distinguished group inside a society that has moved beyond the need for heroes, wherein this group would establish and uphold antiquated principles for its own development.[81]

However, Bohnert also acknowledges that the conflict between prioritizing practicality and efficiency is not a novel concept, as it is already addressed in the Himmeroder Memorandum (1950). This memorandum outlines the internal structure of a prospective German contingent for the defense of Europe, which is disconnected from the military requirements specified in the memorandum. This Himmeroder conflict, which can be understood as an enduring polarization that remains unsolved, was vigorously contested and, somewhat dismissively, referred to as the "founding compromise" of the Bundeswehr. The vehemence of the debate becomes evident when considering that Wolf von Baudissin's ultimate threat to withhold his signature on the undisclosed final document.[82] The intensity of the ongoing discourse between the male and, -more recently, female- representatives of Sparta and Athens within the contemporary Bundeswehr may have subsided with time, although the underlying conflict remains unresolved in the annals of our military history. Politicians advocate for a strategic stance and, as exemplified in the coalition paper of the German government in 2021, places a significant emphasis on Inner Leadership. In contrast, the soldier prioritizes the ability to do their duties with efficiency and professionalism. It is evident that *both* democratic and military importance are inherent in both entities; they are imperative and should be embraced and practiced by all members of the Bundeswehr.

The objective of Inner Leadership is to establish a connection between the two valid perspectives inside opposing demands and reconcile the "two sides a medal."[83] The unity referred to here is not contingent upon a sequential arrangement, where one side is prioritized over the other, resulting in a simple alignment. Rather, it is rooted in an *inherent shared essence.* To express it in a more direct manner: Not first the military training during the week and the Inner Leadership principles just before the end of the day, but also not the political debate, in order to only persuade the soldier to adopt a position after

---

[80] Uwe Hartmann, *Der gute Soldat. Politische Kultur und soldatisches Selbstverständnis heute* (Berlin: Miles-Verlag, 2018), p.89.
[81] Cf. op. cit. Hartmann, pp. 88-94.
[82] Cf. Detlef Bald, „Die gespaltene Ausrichtung der Bundeswehr", *Sicherheit und Frieden*, 2005, pp-177-179.
[83] Bohnert, *Innere Führung auf dem Prüfstand,* p.149.

a lengthy discussion without allowing them to deploy. It is imperative that the legitimate worries of all individuals are acknowledged, comprehended, effectively conveyed, and thereafter put into action by all parties involved. The subsequent section will elucidate the individuals who may experience a heightened sense of relevance and personal connection to the content presented herein.

3.2   Unification of opposites in the person of the superior

The fundamental topic of Friedrich Schiller's work revolves around the *irreconcilability of opposites*, a concept that is not influenced by military considerations. In the context of Inner Leadership, Schiller's thoughts can offer potential solutions. Schiller, whose contributions are somewhat eclipsed by his literary works, showed his versatility as a playwright and poet, while also making significant theoretical contributions in the aftermath of the French Revolution. He adopts a pedagogical and political perspective[84], wherein he examines the distinction between physical necessity, here referred to as "efficiency", and moral necessity, which encompasses democratic values. Schiller indeed posits a hierarchy wherein moral considerations supersede physical ones, a notion that can be comprehended easily given that every action is preceded by an act of valuing. The hierarchical structure maintains a consistent arrangement across the domains of private, professional, and military sectors. I possess a specific objective that I aspire to achieve, and in pursuit of this aim, I have deliberately selected the appropriate strategies and methods.

An army's goal and mission are typically determined by politics. The goal was and is given to the armed forces of this world, with the exception of military coups, and they have the task of advising on the means or choosing them themselves and implementing them in reality (physically), regardless of whether the promotion of internationalism or the "living space in the East" was the aim. Totalitarian governments are simple to operate; their aim is conquest via all means, including violence. In a democracy, it becomes challenging when freedom and the rule of law are prioritized, morality in the sense of Schiller is at risk, and implementing these goals would require using violent military tactics.

This presents a challenge to the soldier in three dimensions. Firstly, the soldier employs force, while simultaneously being subject to limitations on their own freedoms. Additionally, the soldier imposes restrictions on their subordinates through orders and commands, thereby curtailing their freedom or

---

[84] Cf. Schiller, *Über die ästhetische Erziehung des Menschen in einer Reihe von Briefen.*, Letter 2-4, pp. 5-15.

even nullifying it temporarily. - Bundeswehr soldiers have always been aware of this difficulty. Nevertheless, due to the soldier's typical lack of inclination towards engaging in elaborate discussions, the importance of this requirement for the public worker was (too often) taken for granted in previous eras. This has now changed, politicians are taking a closer look and the soldier, who has been educated in school, family and society to be an individual, is asking sharper questions. This automatically puts Inner Leadership "on the spot" and requires it to defend the tried and tested and place it in a new context.

Schiller, similar to Bohnert, also establishes dichotomous relationships in his writing. One of the aforementioned concepts that has been previously discussed is the relationship between physis and morality. Additionally, it is necessary to consider the interplay between *emotion* and *reason*, as well as the dichotomy between *matter* and *spirit*. However, further exploration of these concepts will not be undertaken in this context. The crucial aspect is in the imperative for the political artist to establish a *cohesive synthesis between disparate and opposing elements*, while exercising independent thought and action. This is due to the existence and inherent rationality of all aforementioned components, albeit regrettably giving rise to an enduring paradox. According to Schiller, the artist in question possesses the remarkable capacity to navigate convoluted paths with unwavering rectitude, so earning the designation of a *global citizen* who has elevated his own status via his exceptional talents. *The individual is characterized as the entity in which opposing forces converge, enabling the establishment of a connection and harmonious coalescence due to their inherent participation in all aspects.*

The observation that in an ideal scenario, every soldier may be observed in this global citizen does not elicit astonishment.. However, the focus of attention is often placed towards superiors, as they bear a distinct level of responsibility. In his study, Colonel (ret.) Hannes Wendroth[85] astutely highlights the fundamental premise underlying the method of delegation, which posits that managerial procedures culminate with the individual in a position of authority. Specifically, Wendroth emphasizes the notion that "individuals bear accountability for the outcomes transpiring within their designated sphere of responsibility. The delegation of partial respnsibility is feasible, however the assignment of entire responsibility is not possible.[86]" The Centre for Inner Leadership within the Bundeswehr has a longstanding tradition of

---

[85] Colonel (retired) Hannes Wendroth served until 2015 as the commander of the Schleswig-Holstein State Command. Since then, he has been immersed in executive leadership management.

[86] Wendroth, *Gute Führung - (k)ein Selbstgänger. Kleine Führungshilfe mit praktischen Hinweisen und persönlichen Anmerkungen*, p.53.

prioritizing its attention on the various levels of command within the Bundeswehr, specifically emphasizing the roles of chiefs, company leaders, and commanders.[87] It is plausible, based on the findings from Schiller, common observations, and military structures, that the *individual* represents the sole locus or embodiment capable of *reconciling* and *resolving* conflicts. This is due to their *active engagement* in the tensions between freedom and constraint, life's pleasures and challenges, and the political rationality and military imperatives inherent in their roles as both a citizen and a soldier.

However, the question of how an individual might accomplish this without deviating from the realm of logic has not yet been taken into account. It is apparent that there exist varying circumstances, analogous to the presence of both competent and less competent individuals in positions of authority. Nevertheless, the inherent inconsistencies in the material, akin to the enigmatic task of squaring a circle, persist within the individual and cannot be reconciled when the company commander exhibits a military disposition during morning training, a civic demeanor during afternoon instruction, and an individualistic attitude in the evening. The assumption serves as a unifying factor, much like the metal from which both sides of a coin are composed. The prerequisite and crucial factor in the unification of opposing elements is in the superior's ability to comprehend and deeply grasp the intricacies of this complexity. It is imperative for them to thoroughly examine, assess, and evaluate each instant inside the contradictory and somewhat unique existence of their organization. Currently, there is no individual available to undertake this task on his behalf throughout the time of his decision-making. This represents a *pivotal moment of exceptional intellectual* prowess on his part. In accordance with Schiller's description, this is where he has the opportunity to demonstrate his artistic abilities.

---

[87] In a recent analysis, Meike Wanner provided an account of the extent to which the concept of Inner Leadership is disseminated among the various hierarchical levels within the Bundeswehr. The researcher's findings can be interpreted in two different ways. A significant proportion of enlisted people (78%) and non-commissioned officers (65%) possess limited or negligible knowledge on the concept of Inner Leadership. According to the data, a significant majority of non-commissioned officers (66%), officers (84%), and staff officers (88%) possess knowledge of Inner Leadership or have engaged with it extensively. It is of utmost importance that all individuals in positions of authority pertaining to personnel demonstrate exemplary performance in their evaluations. The presence of staff officers who have not been influenced by Inner Leadership is a cause for concern, as it raises questions about their level of engagement and commitment. Cf. Wanner, „Innere Führung – Philosophie der Streitkräfte oder bloße Anleitung zur Menschenführung?", p. 158.

3.3 Complementary contradictions unite the opposite

While the concept of reconciling opposing elements inside an individual may appear compelling, it is important to acknowledge the substantial disparities that persist between peace and conflict, freedom and compulsion, and right and wrong. However, we are fortunate: from an epistemological standpoint, it can be argued that there exist inherent similarities among opposites due to their *complimentary* nature. It is imperative to provide a thorough explanation and substantiation in order to transcend the realm of personal philosophy and advance the current stage of reasoning.

The concept that opposites are complementary, meaning they mutually influence, mold, and define one another, to the extent that one cannot exist without the other, can be traced back to Hegel's notion of identity as presented in his work titled "The Difference Between Fichte's and Schelling's System of Philosophy (the 'Differenzschrift')" (1801).[88] It becomes evident that *an individual's sense of self inherently implies a distinction from others.* In this context, Hegel addresses mathematical equations, specifically the equation "I = no other". However, it is important to note that the concept of self-identification as "the not-other" is contingent upon the presence of an external entity. This principle is also applicable to all elements comprising the Inner Leadership framework. *The concept of freedom is inherently defined by its limitations, as these restrictions serve as a contrasting element that aids in delineating the nature of freedom. This is due to the fact that freedom cannot be comprehensively understood solely by its own self-explanation.* The notion of morality and immorality is equivalent. The present line of reasoning has the potential for further elaboration within the framework of *negative dialectics,* a concept that is also explored by Adorno and other scholars.

In this context, the concept of *professionalism* can be effectively aligned with the realm of *politics.* Applied to the Bundeswehr as a democratic military force, the temporary restriction of freedom and essential democratic rights during deployment, which I must impose on the troops as their superior, myself, and the enemy, indicates that I cherish liberty and justice. Goals should be kept in mind in the present moment to reinforce them for the future. The *consensus* that is necessary, particularly in the context of a superior, is achieved by a *comprehensive understanding and careful evaluation* of opposing perspectives, ultimately leading to its manifestation. The soldiers possess knowledge of their leader because to their shared comradeship, which is fostered by leading by example and effective communication. Consequently, they also possess an understanding of the reasons behind the limitations imposed on their freedom. The intention is not to permanently deprive individuals of their possessions,

---

[88] Georg Wilhelm Friedrich Hegel, *Differenz des Fichteschen und Schellingschen Systems (kurz: Differenzschrift)* (Leipzig: Reclam, 1981), p.85ff.

but rather to temporarily limit their access to them as a result of unfavorable conditions and to ensure their preservation for future use. Levinas will show that this is a genuine service of the soldier to mankind. Currently, it can be asserted that Inner Leadership has the capacity to fully manifest its potential when comprehended in terms of its inherent contradictions and its supplementary aspect. This also and especially applies to deployments. Regrettably, the quantification of this comprehension is unattainable; yet it can be perceptibly encountered through the presence of an effective leader.

The extent to which the opponent possesses knowledge of the rationale for the temporary curtailment of their freedom, rights, and the consequential jeopardy to their life and well-being may be subject to uncertainty. However, it is both feasible and imperative for the military and political leadership to provide an elucidation to the adversary in this regard. It is anticipated that the current adversaries will potentially evolve into future collaborators. The process of evaluating different perspectives, which may be effectively conveyed to a wide audience, can also be extended to a broader context. This has demonstrated to the German population, in particular, the significance of constraining their freedom as a nation that has previously engaged in aggressive actions. Hence, the United States' involvement in the Second World War, which was met with varying degrees of support, entailed significant responsibilities for the soldiers and the utilization of military force against the aggressor. These actions can be argued to have been grounded in values that align with the principles elucidated in Inner Leadership, thereby providing a democratic justification. The ultimate objective was to establish a lasting peace and facilitate the reestablishment of a democratic Germany. The utilization of force, as implied by Brugmann's initial comment, does not necessarily need to conflict with the democratic structure of the state. Individuals who engage in democratic decision-making consistently incorporate the perspectives of their opponents, as they possess a genuine inclination towards them as individuals and prioritize the welfare of their nation, aligning with their established traditions and usual way of life.

Religiously motivated conflicts, which will only be briefly alluded to in this discussion, can be further elucidated by considering the utilization of violence. This can be attributed to the fact that the three major Abrahamic religions place significant emphasis on the concept of divine mercy, which is believed to be exemplified by certain actions. The necessity of restraining individuals who exhibit ruthlessness is a widely acknowledged concept, and this understanding is commonly derived from one's religious self-perception.

The fulfillment of Inner Leadership's job, particularly in recent years, is not only demonstrated (which may be perceived as resistant to change), but also possesses the ability to cultivate a democratic armed force within the described conditions and philosophical underpinnings. Even within the three manifestations of limiting personal freedom and employing coercive measures, it perceives itself as adhering to democratic principles and embodying liberal values. The Bundeswehr can take pride in its accomplishments, provided it remains steadfast in its commitment to not succumb to superficial, purportedly pacifist perspectives. Such viewpoints are often espoused by those who lack a comprehensive understanding of the dialectical and fluctuating nature inherent in the pursuit of freedom and the safeguarding of democracy.

3.4   Defending Democracy as Identity in the Other

France is a focal point of attention due to the presence of Emmanuel Levinas (1905-1995), who offers a unique perspective on personal *identity* and the *constraints* imposed by the other, particularly within the military context. This perspective, although unfamiliar to us, holds significant value. Levinas posits that the relationship between oneself and the other within a society is perceived as a moral duty incumbent upon the individual, primarily due to the mere presence of the other. Evading this responsibility would entail self-denial and hinder the process of self-realization. Self-awareness is an ongoing process of attaining awareness, which consequently leads to the development of consciousness regarding others. According to Levinas, the relationship between individuals is not solely based on mutual dependency, but rather it is a *complex interconnection* where each person becomes a "hostage" to the other.[89] The primary aim of a democrat, particularly a one who espouses democracy in a specialized role while wearing a uniform, should not encompass the act of shirking obligations towards others or oneself. The subject under consideration exhibits a tendency to neglect the welfare of both themselves and others, as they are unable to attain personal development without adopting obligations.

Levinas further elaborates on the notion of an independent subject that exists in a state of inherent existence, hence establishing a proclivity to relate all occurrences to its own self: The acknowledgment of the presence of others acts as a catalyst for my understanding that my quest for personal freedom is fundamentally egocentric and has negative consequences for the welfare of others. This leads to the emergence of an ethical claim put out by the opposing side, to which I have constantly abided. The individual is assigned the responsibility of adopting accountability for others, wherein their focus on personal well-being is anticipated to transition into a focus on the well-being

---

[89] Cf. Emmanuel Lévinas, *Jenseits des Seins oder anders als Sein geschieht (1978)*, übers. von Thomas Wiemer, 2. Aufl. (Freiburg i.Br: Verlag Karl Alber, 1998), p.248.

of others. As individuals develop a more profound comprehension of their own being, there is a corresponding tendency to surrender personal agency. This procedure results in a heightened acknowledgment of individual responsibility. "The more I come to myself, the more I lay down my freedom (...), the more I discover myself responsible; the more righteous I am, the more guilty I am.[90]" According to the philosopher Levinas, who makes explicit reference to the works of Hegel, the concept of the "other" is understood as the other self. The distinctiveness of this French philosopher lies in his employment of a very forceful vocabulary that effectively aligns with the subject matter and many challenging realities. Therefore, it aptly illustrates the profound vocation of the soldier in the battlefield.

The democratic leader voluntarily limits their personal liberties and expects the same level of restraint from their military personnel. Conversely, they reciprocate this action against their adversary. The soldier (= subject), in this context, assumes the burden of guilt on behalf of others or is required to bear its consequences. This implies that the soldier is held captive by a sense of responsibility, whereby they are blamed or held accountable for the actions or sufferings of others. "The subject is hostage insofar as it is possessed by responsibility, (...) Which means concretely: (Everyone is) accused of what the others do or suffer, or responsible for what the others do or suffer. The uniqueness of the I consists precisely in this: to bear the guilt of the others[91]".

The soldiers of the Bundeswehr play a crucial role in *bearing* the democratic principles of the state. Consequently, the soldier assumes the responsibility for the other, an individual whose presence is integral to the soldier's development as a person, thereby giving rise to sentiments of appreciation and obligation, particularly towards the citizens of the homeland. However, this also assumes a distinct approach towards acknowledging their errors and feelings of guilt, particularly in relation to military conflicts. This is due to the fact that every instance of armed conflict is typically preceded by a series of mistakes, as well as a failure to prevent or actively pursue non-violent alternatives. This perspective significantly influences the professional mindset of soldiers, particularly in high-risk situations, and is aligned with the principles of Inner Leadership.

The indispensable function of a soldier within a democratic society is in their capacity to provide assistance to other citizens and assume accountability for errors. This allows individuals to offer suitable answers to the *three fundamental inquiries of Inner Leadership*, as delineated at the initiation of the framework. A

---

[90] Op. cit. Lévinas. p. 249. The term "guilty" in this context does not refer to experiencing guilt, but rather is used in a causal sense to describe the obligations one has towards others.

[91] Op. cit. Lévinas, p.248.

noteworthy characteristic of this technique resides in its ability to theoretically tackle inquiries, particularly within the domain of ideal conceptualization. The concept of *collaboration* within the Bundeswehr is generally perceived as a form of service, distinguished by a mutual sense of obligation. The intrinsic talent of each human enables them to absorb strange and challenging concepts on an individual level. By engaging in this practice, individuals are able to achieve personal autonomy in a thoughtful manner and acknowledge the importance of their own existence in relation to others. In this particular environment, the Bundeswehr serves as more than just a fundamental element of *society*; it also serves as a symbol of a democratic and responsible nation. As a result, the German Armed Forces are widely seen as an essential establishment of the state, since it encapsulates the ideals and doctrines that enable it to be acknowledged and supported by society as an emblematic representation of the nation. The Bundeswehr's possession of humility and dedication to its duties bestow upon it the inherent legitimacy required to effectively carry out its job.[92]

The foundation and manifestation of all theoretical concepts are rooted in the cognitive, affective, and behavioral processes of the immediate supervisor. The individual in question assumes the role of single possessor and enforcer of Inner Leadership, regularly exhibiting this capability when they have a thorough understanding of, deliberate about, and effectively manage military actions. Hence, there exists no justification for the establishment of a *distinct Inner Leadership entity for operations*. Furthermore, there exists a potential risk that certain distinctive attributes may be subjected to regulation in such a context, which upon deeper scrutiny, may ultimately prove to be idiosyncratic in nature. Individuals and collectives who perceive themselves as possessing exclusive and exceptional qualities have historically exhibited a propensity towards eccentric behavior.[93] The potential consequences described here would similarly pose a risk to the distinct Inner Leadership within specific groups and tasks. This publication aims to provide evidence for the Inner Leadership for democratic armed forces across all areas of responsibility, rendering any extra elements superfluous and counterproductive. - In addition to theoretical considerations, it is important to emphasize that during critical moments of decision-making, particularly when faced with time constraints and hazardous circumstances, the guidance provided by regulations alone is insufficient. Instead, the superior's ability to make informed judgments based on their broad education becomes crucial in effectively

---

[92] At this juncture, it is imperative to make reference to the fifth axiom. The foundation for comprehending this axiom is in the examination and response to the guiding questions put forward by the philosophy of Emanuel Levinas.

[93] Cf. Immanuel Kant, *Anthropologie in pragmatischer Hinsicht*. (Königsberg, 1798), p.7.

navigating complex circumstances. It is imperative to allocate the superior significant focus, as they necessitate professional military training, comprehensive understanding of the intricate interrelationships and inherent tensions within democratic armed forces, and the embodiment of this information in their daily life. Furthermore, it is imperative to minimize any sources of disturbance that may impede their mental clarity, so allowing their mind to be unburdened. This is crucial as it is the intellect that propels actions and influences outcomes.

4   The five axioms of Inner Leadership

Thus far, the notion of axioms has been explored within the works of Blaise Pascal, Paul Watzlawick, and to a lesser extent, Sven Lange, primarily within the realm of humanities. The scientific disciplines of mathematics and physics have thus far received insufficient attention, and this trend is expected to persist due to the potential for an unproductive expansion of the topic.

The examination of the Inner Leadership of the Bundeswehr has been approached in an unconventional manner so far, particularly due to the inclusion of previously overlooked authors in this domain. It is now opportune to culminate these deliberations by designating axioms and principles derived from prior knowledge, so rendering them applicable to the leadership culture of armed forces of democratic nations.

It is important to approach each premise in a uniform manner, akin to the perspective advocated by Watzlawick. The process of *assigning names* will be accompanied by subsequent *explanations* that draw on the preceding context. These explanations will encompass the main topic and include a concise repetition for emphasis. The inclusion of a historical connection, which has been absent in the preceding text, is deemed necessary. It is prudent to refrain from introducing novel concepts and simultaneously pursuing the historical connection as a concurrent narrative thread.

Nevertheless, it is evident that certain aspects outlined thus far may not be included in previous Inner Leadership literature. In the realm of contemporary politics within Germany, it is evident that not all aspects can be exclusively attributed to the Ahlen or Godesberg program[94]. However, it is important to note that this does not imply a dearth of validity for novel concepts and perspectives. The official Inner Leadership demonstrates a continued adherence to the original principles and ideas put forward by its founding fathers, namely Wolf von Baudissin, Ulrich de Maizière, and to a lesser extent, Johann Adolf Graf von Kielmansegg. This is evident in the selection of vocabulary and the range of subjects addressed. There is a dearth of novel findings, as several research endeavors predominantly focus on historical description and exhibit a reluctance to venture into the realm of conceptual exploration. The reorganization of existing elements does not constitute a novel conceptualization.

However, even the detractors of Inner Leadership failed to present any novel ideas. The stakeholders expressed a need for innovation while dismissing the previous methods as ineffective. Despite the clear call made by Holz, Lange,

---

[94] Prior to the 21st century, the two largest parties in Germany were the social democratic SPD and the Christian conservative CDU. After World War II, each created a basic plan for themselves: The CDU in Ahlen (1947) and the SPD in Bad Godesberg (1959)

and Hartmann for a new approach to Inner Leadership, it is evident that no one has yet heeded their plea.

There exists a pronounced inclination inside the Bundeswehr to establish connections with the progenitors of Inner Leadership. This observation may be attributed to the conventional prominence of military history research, a characteristic that distinguishes it from other disciplines within the humanities. The emergence of recent advancements in Inner Leadership can be attributed to the introduction of novel duties, characterized by a significant administrative nature. These jobs necessitate the completion of specific work at a designated location deemed appropriate for their execution. The rationale behind the necessity for an adjustment of Inner Leadership in response to new duties remains ambiguous. The preservation of purpose fulfillment, legitimation, and the promotion of welfare, as well as the internal behavior and the portrayal of man as peace-oriented, remain unchanged. However, it can be observed that Inner Leadership is currently focused on expanding the range of themes covered. The impact of this expansion on the actual performance of military leadership in practical situations is yet to be determined. The additional responsibilities[95], mentioned by Sven Lange, do not match with the primary aims of Inner Leadership. It is not advisable to build a separate Inner Leadership for each phenomenon. This keeps staff busy and filing cabinets full, but it does little to aid the leader on the ground. Inadequate attention has been paid to the issue, supporting the previously noted tendency toward a *convolute of Inner Leadership.*

In contrast, the axioms aim to provide a theoretical foundation for an idea rooted in the humanities, as exemplified within the framework of this critique. Axioms are self-evident and do not require any argument, hence they are mostly elucidated to enhance their clarity. For this sole reason, they possess the entitlement to be comprehended as a genuine basis upon which individuals can construct.

Significant progress has been made in the development of a concrete concept, leading to a more profound understanding of existing factors. In the course of the conducted investigation, it has been discovered that the writings of the founding fathers of Inner Leadership contain several echoes of the following axioms. The exploration of the historical relationship between the axioms is a highly intriguing endeavor, primarily due to the uncertainty surrounding the compatibility of the recently developed concept of Inner Leadership with the long-standing texts of Baudissin, de Maizière, and

---

[95] Lange mentions structural measures of defense organization, new possibilities of hybrid and asymmetric warfare, political and religious extremism, digitalization, growing diversity and variety

Kielmansegg. The two concepts, have significant similarities, primarily in their alignment, but diverge in terms of linguistic style and the sequence of topics discussed. It is noteworthy that contemporary Inner Leadership predominantly employs the terminology introduced by Baudissin. Count von Kielmansegg, a proficient rhetorician and a thoughtful intellectual, is often overlooked or underestimated.[96]

The elucidation of the study endeavor could be intriguing in order to enhance the transparency of the method. The present study involved an analysis of a collection of essays to ascertain the specific locations within the texts where Axioms I-V are referenced. The satisfactory outcome entails the presence of all axioms within a diverse amalgamation of significant works and speeches pertaining to Inner Leadership. This may be seen as a triumph; nevertheless, it also exposes two inherent limitations within the existing Inner Leadership framework. On one hand, there is a consistent reorganization of content from essay to essay, while on the other, the texts have maintained a manageable extent since their inception. The Bundeswehr has not perpetuated the historical tradition established by Clausewitz, Scharnhorst, and Gneisenau, wherein armed forces commanders and generals engage in the authorship of strategic and conceptual literature. Especially for the area of Inner Leadership Kielmansegg regrets this in his detailed foreword to "Die Bundeswehr in der Demokratie. Zeit der Inneren Führung (1971)" (The Bundeswehr in Democracy. Time of Inner Leadership (1971): "To my great regret, the great demands of the job (...) make it impossible to."[97] Subsequently, a period over 15 years transpired from the establishment of the Bundeswehr to the publication of the inaugural book on Inner Leadership. Prior to it, the existing documentation on Inner Leadership was limited to fragmented references found in various legal documents, such as laws, decrees, rules, protocols, guidelines, and similar sources.

The extent to which Inner Leadership has successfully overcome its initial shortcomings remains a subject of debate. Furthermore, it is worth considering if the persistent inquiry surrounding "Inner Leadership in the crisis?" may be traced back to these early deficiencies. - There is one notable exception, namely, Carl-Gero von Ilsemann's book, which remains relevant and valuable in contemporary times. However, the author himself modestly describes it as "a compendium intended primarily for reference purposes". The

---

[96] Conducting a comprehensive evaluation of Kielmansegg's extensive papers, spanning 16.25 linear meters in the Freiburg Federal Archives, would present a highly valuable research endeavour for Inner Leadership.

[97] Johann-Adolf von Kielmansegg, *Einführung des Herausgebers, Die Bundeswehr in der Demokratie. Zeit der Inneren Führung.* (Hamburg: Decker's Verlag, 1971), rom V.

focus of this analysis is solely on providing a complete descriptive narrative.[98] The absence of discourse regarding substantiation and systematization is evident.

In a very dense essay, Sven Lange introduces the concept of axioms to the world of Inner Leadership.[99] It is mentioned in the already alluded essay "Fit für das 21. Jahrhundert" (Fit for the 21st Century), where the author dwells on the historical, yet the detailed look is worthwhile:[100] Lange initiates the discussion by highlighting that Inner Leadership was specifically designed to cater to the social requirements of the newly established Federal Republic. The Weimar Republic's failure and the subsequent collapse of the Third Reich were significant historical events that were experienced during that period. The emergence of the "Handbuch der Inneren Führung" (Manual of Inner Leadership) can be traced back to its initial publication in 1957, under the authorship of Inspector General Heusinger. This publication aimed to elucidate the fundamental principles, duties, objectives, and methodologies associated with the concept of Inner Leadership. It is important to note that this manual was not intended as a prescriptive guide, but rather as a resource for reading and study purposes. Given that Lange's usage of the term "axioms" is solely present in the title, it can be inferred that the text pertains to fundamental concepts, such as "duty to preserve freedom" and "obedience out of insight," which the author perceives as axiomatic. However, it is important to note that these principles are specifically applicable to a conscript army. Lange's explanation of the term 'axiom' lacks specificity and fails to provide a clear definition. Based on the given context, it may be inferred that these terms are employed interchangeably with the concepts of "fundamentals" or "linchpins" within the framework of Inner Leadership.

Currently, there is a lack of axioms that are derived from philosophical principles rather than being dependent on the specific historical lessons of individual countries in the recent past. The subsequent discussion will address their inclusion and assert their applicability to not only the German armed forces, but also to the armed forces of any democratic nation.

Nevertheless, it is important to note that the extensive disassociation of the leadership culture within the armed forces from the historical context of a state, as suggested in this statement, is unlikely to receive widespread acceptance in the foreseeable future. However, this does not exclude the formulation of such a concept as an ideal.

---

[98] op. cit. von Kielmansegg.rom. VI.

[99] see chap. 2.2

[100] Cf. Lange, „Fit für das 21. Jahrhundert: Warum die Konzeption der Inneren Führung eine neue Meistererzählung benötigt", pp. 36-41.

The subsequent five ideals (axioms) possess practical importance and are not abstract concepts originating solely from the intellectual confines of scholarly research. In contemporary discourse, it has become common to liken an ideal to a lighthouse, a metaphor that holds significant utility. This metaphor serves to highlight a focal point that embodies a solid and justified objective, as opposed to a fleeting notion that may initially appear valid but is ultimately proven elusive. Furthermore, this metaphor emphasizes the feasibility of realizing and incorporating this objective into one's daily endeavors. Not consistently on a daily basis, but rather repeatedly and frequently.

4.1   First Axiom

Motivated by ideals - **The foundation of a democratic military rests on assumptions that cannot be guaranteed by either the state or the military.** - *Values in society*

A discernible sequence is evident. The individuals within a society play a crucial role in shaping the state and its constitution. Their attitudes and values serve as the foundation upon which the state is built. Once these principles are established and incorporated into the legal framework, it becomes imperative to safeguard this community and its legal system, both from internal and external threats. It depends on which "spirit"[101] inspires the community. It is evident as well the fundamental laws the entity establishes for itself, and which regulations govern its military personnel.

The Federal Republic of Germany, particularly in its early years, can be effectively illustrated in comparison to other nations. Notably, specific milestones can be identified to support this assertion. This assertion potentially pertains to the constitutional validity of the state and its safeguarding against external threats. Let us reflect upon the historical significance of two key events: May 24, 1949, which marked the entry into force of the Basic Law, and November 12, 1955, which witnessed the establishment of the Bundeswehr. However, this immediately shifts the focus on the outcomes rather than the underlying conditions. The constitution was desired by the populace of West Germany, reflecting a blend of legal tradition, legal expertise, and the legal sensitivities of a state that has developed its federal tradition over an extended duration. The Basic Law, frequently invoked by the Inner Leadership as a fundamental basis, is not merely a monolithic legal endowment, but rather an outcome. The phenomenon has emerged from the inherent essence of the nation, which exists outside the realm of legal regulations, so rendering the stability of law constantly at risk, susceptible to the whims of change. Disinterest, left-wing and right-wing extremism, Islamism and sectarian moralism that rises above the law are probably the greatest current threats to the spirit of responsibility, consideration and balance that should unite the citizens and nationals of our country.

Similar ideas can be observed in Kielmansegg's speech delivered on July 20, 1963 at the Beethovenhalle in Bonn.[102] The moral conscience exhibited by the individuals involved in the events of July 20, 1944, serves as a justification for their violation of established laws and a perverted oath. It asserts its

---

[101] Wolf Wilhelm Friedrich von Baudissin, *Grundwert Frieden*, hg. von Claus Freiherr von Rosen (Berlin: Miles-Verlag, 2014), p.290.

[102] Cf. Johann-Adolf von Kielmansegg, „Der deutsche Soldat und der 20. Juli", *Festschrift zum sechzigsten Geburtstag*, 1966, pp.53ff.

position in front of legal principles and holds itself superior to an illegitimate legal framework. The decision holds the highest legal priority as a judgment based on ethical knowledge. The legal priority is extended to every soldier, while nevertheless maintaining the militarily required hierarchy and requirement of obedience. "In the occidental legal sphere we find that the right of resistance against the law-breaking ruler was and is recognized almost everywhere and always. This recognition, even codification, has found practically no interruption in the states of Anglo-Saxon law and also in Denmark until today, but on the continent in the age of absolutism, whereby it came to life again in France by the revolution of 1789 and has remained alive. (...) (Moreover, there was) a fully developed medieval right of resistance (...), grown out of the three roots of an already pre-medieval Germanic folk law, a feudal right of resistance of the feudal state, and a right of resistance developed by the church.[103]" Notably, this doctrine even superseded the divine forgiveness. Kielmansegg (1966) also refers to the "Strasbourg Oaths" and the Carolinian state treaty of 842. These historical events are of particular significance to the military personnel involved, since they entailed the swearing of an oath of allegiance to their monarch, which may be nullified in the event of a violation of royal law.[104] - It is evident from this observation that each individual has an inherent moral compass that has been bestowed upon them from ancient times, leading to the formation of conscientious choices. The potential inclusion of the emergence of a comprehensive legal system through a constitutional process is a logical consideration. However, Kielmansegg's omission of this aspect in their discourse may be attributed to the speech's focus on military resistance, which may have rendered a discussion on such a large topic impractical.

The existence of written laws and the constitution is contingent upon the actions of individuals, making them the ultimate agents of legal authority. Hence, it is imperative for a democratic military institution to align itself with the governing state. Furthermore, it is imperative for the entity to possess an understanding that its existence is reinforced by the confidence and determination of its populace to safeguard it. Furthermore "promoting mutual understanding of the different tasks and structures of a free constitutional state and pluralistic society on the one hand and effective and reliable armed forces through obedience on the other is part of the special task and responsibility of the Inspector General.[105]" The historical justification for this conclusion

---

[103]Op. cit.von Kielmansegg. p. 55.
[104] Cf. op. cit.

[105] Ernst Wagemann, *Fortwirkende Impulse für die „Innere Führung", Stationen eines Soldatenlebens* (Bonn: Mittler und Sohn, 1982), p.108.

is seen in the figure of Ulrich de Maizière. In 1982, Eberhard Wagemann, a former Major General, compiled "continuing Impulses for Inner Leadership." - The preservation of the constitutional state is contingent upon the armed forces possessing a disposition that is both open-minded and inclusive. The disposition of the populace plays a pivotal role in shaping the nature of the military forces. Consequently, these individuals who are united in their mindset cannot tolerate a situation where certain factions within the military do not possess the same mindset.

The notion of "reciprocity" may appear innocuous; however, it possesses significant influence. When the legal entity, specifically society, refuses to acknowledge the armed force's role in providing external security or fails to support it, society undermines the armed forces, leaving them disoriented and weak. Consequently, society becomes vulnerable to the uncertainties that lie ahead in an unpredictable future. In his written work titled " „Bekenntnis zum Soldaten" (Confession of the Soldier) Wagemann cites de Maizière:[106] "For the military defense of a democracy cannot dispense with the will to defend of the individual citizen of a nation, nor with the proficiency of the troops.[107]"

This quote underscores the former Inspector General's particular focus on the incorporation of the Bundeswehr into the civilian society. The publication titled "Führen im Frieden" (Leading in Peace), written by the retired former Inspector General in 1974, adheres consistently to this established pattern.[108] The author initially examines the legal underpinnings of the Federal Republic as a whole, with a specific focus on the Bundeswehr. In undertaking this endeavor, the individual commences by referencing the Basic Law and maintains unwavering adherence to its principles throughout the process. The author's expository sections possess a descriptive quality, since they elucidate the state of affairs rather than *delving into the underlying causes*. He does not consider the will of the people to be a persuasive factor. The aforementioned impression has manifested itself inside the realm of law, establishing its validity and obviating the necessity for more elucidation. The legal-ethical certainty associated with Protestantism offers limited assistance in providing a justifiable rationale. Individuals must get a thorough understanding of the material and accept the knowledge as an intrinsic part of their personal identity before acting in accordance with their newly acquired knowledge.

---

[106] Ulrich de Maiziere, *Bekenntnis zum Soldaten. Militärische Führung in unserer Zeit.* (Hamburg: R. v. Deckers Verlag, 1972), pp.186f.

[107] op. cit. Wagemann.p. 114.

[108] Ulrich de Maiziere, *Führen im Frieden* (München: Bernard und Graefe, 1974).

To establish the robust basis of this concept, it is imperative to reference the scholarly work of Wolf von Baudissin. "There has always been unanimity among us (i.e. Baudissin, de Maizière and Kielmansegg, *Author's note*.) There has always been unanimity that the soldierly order must be a congruent part of the overall order. Armies can only be in shape if they reflect the structure of the whole and if they are inspired by the same spirit that sustains the whole."[109] The choice of the phrase "inspired by the spirit" by Baudissin, rather than "united by the same legal order," appears to be of significant importance in relation to the alignment with the first axiom. The will to the State, its constitution, and its defense emanates from the collective consciousness of both the State and the community. The armed forces rely on this spirit.

The essence of Inner Leadership, extending beyond the formalities of legal documentation, has been previously acknowledged in relation to the examination of the axioms. The coexistence of an excess and a deficiency of laws is a perpetual phenomenon. Too many to know at the moment of the decision and too few to regulate the individual case in the specific situation. The sole path to achieving superiority is in the consistent practice of everyday service, which fosters the development of a particular mindset characterized by critical thinking and the ability to synthesize information.

Legal and ethical arguments often fail to provide definitive solutions to particular inquiries. The utilization of a singular methodological approach and the employment of legal terminology in the works of Ulrich de Maizière is particularly noteworthy.[110] It is evident that the adoption of the modular language of Inner Leadership occurred no later than the early 1970s, as evidenced by the writings of Ilsemann and de Maizière. This language, which continues to be prevalent in numerous publications, is officially documented as a term file at the Centre for Innere Führung in the German Armed Forces. Kielmansegg was essentially amused by it from the beginning, as evidenced by his description of Ilsemann's book as a "compendium for reference"[111]; this is essentially a house tour of the Centre of Inner Leadership in Coblenz, Germany: this is where one can see this and that; one system functions in a particular way, while another system functions slightly differently. Nevertheless, as previously said, Inner Leadership lacks a reference to comprehensiveness, which ultimately gives rise to the potential for arbitrary reasoning. This is primarily because the house tour can be conducted in many manners, leading to a lack of consistency in the argumentation. This phenomenon

---

[109] von Baudissin, *Grundwert Frieden*, p.290.
[110] Cf. op. cit. von Baudissin, pp.136ff.
[111] von Kielmansegg, „Einführung", rom. VI.

elicits disquiet among warriors who possess independent thinking abilities. Concurrently, there exists a perception among certain individuals that this establishment has assumed the role of the revered Grail Castle of Inner Leadership, a sentiment that can be comprehended.[112] The aforementioned approach carries implications due to *its adherence to traditional modular reasoning, which prioritizes legal ethics and neglects to engage conceptually with the perspectives of individuals and events. For individuals to engage in debate, it is necessary to possess a structured framework that does not necessitate further validation.*

Moreover, it is important to acknowledge that Kielmansegg's metaphor pertaining to the domicile, the architectural layout, and the diverse rooms aligns remarkably with the concept denoted as "Convolut." The issues addressed by Inner Leadership, which are said to be diverse and expanding in number, are structured in a manner reminiscent of the rooms of a house. The contemplation of the five axioms of Inner Leadership involves the transfer of Inner Leadership from its historical context to a more streamlined and efficient setting, akin to a Tiny House. This environment allows individuals to readily access and utilize their five tools, enabling them to live harmoniously and contentedly.

---

[112] Cf. Bohnert, *Innere Führung auf dem Prüfstand,* pp. 35, 86ff.

4.2 Second Axiom

Called to Freedom. **The Inner Leadership of a Democratic Armed Force will always be relevant.** - *The Value of Democracy*

Individuals who endeavor to remain current must acknowledge the presence of three inherent drawbacks, which are not always indicative of an unwillingness to adjust, but rather arise from logical reasoning.

1.   If you want to keep up with the times, you are always behind it.

This statement conceals certain incomplete truths that warrant careful consideration. The concept of time, when conceptualized as a duration, necessitates definition and analysis due to its fleeting nature. This process is inherently intricate and hence requires a considerable amount of time to be undertaken. The significance of highlighting a seemingly inactive system within many democratic forces is negligible. The multifaceted nature of the issue at hand is evident when considering many factors such as political will, geopolitical context, societal norms, individual preferences, and military considerations. Consequently, it becomes apparent that finding straightforward solutions to this complicated scenario is a challenging endeavor.

The comprehension of 'contemporaneity' requires a considerable level of discursive proficiency, as it is the participants' collective skill that ultimately determines what is considered contemporary. This observation highlights the challenging circumstances that Inner Leadership and the on-site supervisor may encounter. The identification and implementation of practical solutions that garner widespread agreement in this context might be considered a remarkable manifestation of rationality.

The ongoing events in the conflict between Russia and Ukraine exemplify the rapidity with which circumstances can evolve. In a relatively short period of time, significant transformations have occurred on a global scale, particularly in Europe and other regions. The current era has witnessed significant transformations. - A leadership structure that is internally oriented and aligned with the current context would exhibit little responsiveness. One could argue, with a discernible expression of amusement, that the previous iteration of Inner Leadership, frequently criticized for its inability to fulfill the demands of the operational army, is inadequate for the current undertaking. The oversight is in neglecting to consider the timing of the army of global missions, which had autonomously departed and afterwards returned to the country and the alliance.

2.   If you want to keep up with the times, you are responsive.

The point has already been addressed in the preceding statement. What is the purpose of familiarizing oneself with the concept of the contemporary? A hierarchical relationship is established in this context. The tone is not determined by the well-established principles of Inner Leadership, but rather by the contextual factors and circumstances of the era. The previous paragraph highlighted the intricate dynamics that contribute to the formation of the zeitgeist within a specific timeframe, emphasizing its inherent unpredictability. It is advised not to rely on this phenomenon under any circumstances. Leadership that is primarily driven by the perceived need for prompt action might be considered inadequate and lacking in true leadership qualities.

The reason for Inner Leadership's consistent reclamation of the contemporary is not just attributable to its surrounding context. The establishment of the entity in question can be attributed to its emergence as a response to the errors committed during the Nazi era, with a special focus on the actions of the Wehrmacht. The Himmerode Memorandum was evidently a product of the perspective that "such a state of affairs must not persist." This phenomenon can be readily seen in light of the complexities arising from the ongoing conflict. Nevertheless, it is imperative to acknowledge that this emergence can be attributed to a pessimistic impetus, since it explicitly articulated our aversion towards certain objectives. The prevailing sentiment during that period was undeniably appropriate, potentially being the sole feasible approach, and Inner Leadership was unable to undergo systematic development due to time constraints. Its creation is a result of the collaboration between intellectually astute individuals with a deep understanding of democratic principles and military expertise. However, its design is intended to be responsive in nature, as evidenced by its structure. If the current state persists indefinitely, the perception of a deficient Inner Leadership becomes apparent, relying on the "signs of the times" to discern its objectives. Consequently, the entity in question experiences a decline in its position and becomes reactive, necessitating an explanation for its relevance if its perception of itself lacks sufficient consideration for forthcoming circumstances.

The aforementioned reflections elucidate the rationale behind the highly logical decision to employ the Axioms of Inner Leadership in order to construct a novel critical narrative that effectively showcases the potentialities inherent in Inner Leadership. The reason for the replacement of the old narrative is not due to its obsolescence, but rather stems from the inherent nature of a contemporary Inner Leadership, which gradually becomes obsolete as time progresses. Hence, it is crucial to transition from a chronological perspective to fundamental principles (axioms) that prioritize intellectual and scientific thought, notwithstanding the inherent challenges associated with achieving this objective. The concept appears to possess a somewhat philosophical nature and is not widely recognized or understood. *Organizations that adhere to fundamental concepts and possess personnel that actively apply these principles in their daily operations, thereby leading in accordance with them, will be able to surpass the prevailing trends.* From a logical and practical standpoint, it is evident that there are no alternative methods available.

What is required are a set of axioms and their astute interpretation in specific instances. The use of *judgment is necessary, rather than relying solely on the purported timeliness* of a growing multitude of regulations, instructions, and manuals. The Romans established the twelve-table law, an important legal code that was inscribed on stone tablets and prominently displayed in the forum. This code served as the foundation for legal ideas that were then invoked and expounded upon in court speeches to address specific cases. The focus lies within the realm of Inner Leadership, namely in its axioms, which govern the internal framework of the armed forces through a concise set of fundamental ideas that may be conveniently encapsulated on a pocket-sized card.

3.   If you want to keep up with the times, you are not autonomous.

This subpoint has already been provided in the preceding information. The subject of temporal definition is a significant inquiry that prompts us to consider the authority responsible for establishing the concept of time. In the context of acquired modesty, it is widely acknowledged that the prevailing consensus is that one's focus should primarily be directed towards others. Very few individuals would assert their ability to exert control over contemporary events, yet they see the unfolding circumstances in their immediate surroundings. Nonetheless, the concept of Inner Leadership transcends the scope of any singular individual who engages with it. The subject matter pertains to the fundamental principles of governance and their safeguarding, so rendering the display of false humility inappropriate, but rather necessitating leadership in the context of democracy. In this context, it is imperative to prioritize the establishment and adherence to fundamental norms and ideas, which have become so integral that their justification is no longer necessary. The examination and study of Inner Leadership is encouraged for both state and society.

The purported benefit of determining what is contemporary would be a more precise definition of what is customary and popular in the Bundeswehr. In the realm of Inner Leadership, it is important to note that a false sense of security can be established, as the definition of what is considered contemporary consistently necessitates an overwhelming level of expectation. As Liessmann previously proposed, the term's seeming clarity serves as a conceptual framework within which the interplay between *conformity* and *non-conformity* can be examined.[113] In order to establish a definition of time, it is imperative for individuals to consistently contextualize their understanding within the framework of *their* personal and historical experiences. The

---

[113] Cf. ch. 2.1

illumination of current circumstances is facilitated by an understanding of past challenges, as it is through the distinction from previous conditions that novel developments can emerge. - The open and dialogical leader can establish a position within the psychosocial realm by employing their method of evaluation and guidance, which involves navigating the tension between *maintaining continuity with established practices and making necessary corrections in the present.* It becomes more convenient for an individual if they possess a repertoire of thoughts that is not influenced by time, and if they also have the opportunity and dedication to engage in contemplation.

The current *facet of Inner Leadership lies in the ability to judge in the present moment.* It is imperative to acknowledge that this process of deliberative thought draws upon military-historical patterns. Uwe Hartmann reference the leadership philosophy of Clausewitz, wherein emphasis is placed on the cultivation of a "discerning and perceptive mind, enabling the individual to ascertain the truth through the discerning faculties of their judgment."[114] Only in this way can it be possible to come to grips with the imponderables of waging war. To move mentally active and free in a space of definition is therefore not only crucial for Inner Leadership, but for the task surpassing everything else, namely the successful combat action.

In Inner Leadership, the mental attitude of weighing or oscillating thoughts is no different from that of Clausewitz. *Perhaps this is even the chance for the axioms of Inner Leadership to prevail because they originate from a deeply military-practical attitude of mind, without which there is nothing to be gained not only in human leadership, but also in combat!*

Kielmansegg further emphasizes the following notion: "Similar to how a spear must be crafted with a focus on its tip rather than its shaft, in order to effectively hit its target, the shaft must possess the qualities necessary to provide force and direction to the tip. Similarly, Inner Leadership must not overlook the fundamental principle that an army is 'designed' for its combatants."[115] It is important to note that the defence of a country 's interest, which is the primary objective and purpose of the armed forces, is justified for various reasons. The axioms exhibit no divergence from the established principles of Inner Leadership. In the context of Inner Leadership, the prioritization of individual interests does not supersede the collective whole.

Towards the conclusion of the chapter, it is imperative to acknowledge the influence of the notion of "contemporary" within the context of Inner Leadership as espoused by the founding fathers. The concept of "contemporary leadership" is widely recognized as a fundamental aspect of organizational

---

[114] Uwe Hartmann, *Offiziersbibliothek Deutschland* (Berlin: Miles-Verlag, 2020), pp.84f.
[115] von Kielmansegg, „Einführung", rom XII.(translated by the author)

identity. Is the entirety of this content intended to be deemed incorrect at present? In this context, it is appropriate to provide reassurance, as the term in question has acquired an independent existence and hence necessitated a largely unacknowledged reevaluation. Ultimately, it is noteworthy that each of the three key figures responsible for establishing Inner Leadership has military backgrounds inside either the Reichswehr or the Wehrmacht. Furthermore, they played influential roles in shaping the development of the Bundeswehr during their lifetimes. In this context, a significant shift in the perception of time has occurred, transitioning from a state characterized by demagoguery to one embracing democratic principles. This transformation is marked by a shift from defensive tactics to active engagement, from the imposition of doctrines to the promotion of individuality, and from passive obedience to the recognition and consideration of other perspectives.[116] Over the course of an individual's lifetime, temporal dynamics have undergone transformations, leading to a corresponding rationale for the importance of timeliness. The members of the Bundeswehr, who trace their military heritage back to the National People's Army (NVA), continue to perceive the impact of societal shifts in the present era. The alteration observed in this context pertains not to the temporal dimension, but rather to the fundamental structure of the state system through time.

However, what is currently perceived as crucial for purportedly modern leadership is often nothing more than a disrupted sense of empathy, which fundamentally jeopardizes or even intentionally disregards the operational preparedness of the German armed forces due to excessively prioritized personal agendas. The individual who references purportedly contemporary Inner Leadership in this context distorts and misuses its principles. Baudissin presents a critical perspective on this evaluation: "It should be noted, particularly with regard to unpleasant incidents and occasionally quite alarming violations of the fundamental rules of liberal human leadership, that where free-thinking superiors know their business and identify with our reality and the demands of Inner Leadership, there are surprisingly few frictions and mishaps."[117] This alignment significantly reduces instances of conflict and

---

[116] Nevertheless, the Bundeswehr was able to draw upon the Inner Leadership strategies employed in the Wehrmacht. There existed an implicit norm dictating that individuals in a position of lower authority were to be afforded a certain level of respectful treatment. The derivation of rights from this source is not feasible. Cf. Neitzel, *Deutsche Krieger. Vom Kaiserreich zur Berliner Republik – eine Militärgeschichte*, pp.356-361.

[117] von Baudissin, *Grundwert Frieden,* p.296. In light of the aforementioned remark, it is important to acknowledge that the concept of effective Inner Leadership is multifaceted and requires extensive guidance, meticulous examination, and long-term practice. Based on discussions with young officers, it is suggested that there is a need for a revitalization of New Inner

dysfunction, as evidenced by the contextual interpretation of the quote, even in high-pressure scenarios. Based on that statement, it can be inferred that Baudissin considers *liberal leadership* and *contemporary leadership* to be nearly *interchangeable* terms. This is likely due to the fact that we currently reside in a liberal era following the years 1945 and 1990. Contemporaneity, in this context, does not include blindly adopting trends and societal changes without first evaluating their desirability. It would be highly inappropriate to include these unapproved developments in regulations, decrees, and manuals, as they would continue to be enforced by the system's inertia, despite their proven obsolescence.

To further enhance the correlation between contemporary and unrestricted leadership, a final excerpt from the 1965 award ceremony honoring the three pioneers of Inner Leadership is presented. This encompasses all three individuals, with particular emphasis on Baudissin's direct reference to de Maizière. The crucial aspect to consider in this line of reasoning is the recognition that *contemporaneity does not merely reflect the social events of the present moment, but rather represents the temporalization of timeless principles, particularly those related to freedom.*

"Inner Leadership occurs in a contemporary soldierly leadership that gives the soldier the inner attitude and fortitude to fight with the weapon and in a spiritual armor that prepares him for the spiritual confrontation with the totalitarianism that threatens us."[118] Emphasizing the importance of freedom entails the rejection of totalitarianism, as evidenced by historical experience. Despite superficial alterations in its outward manifestations, linguistic preferences, or geographical variations, totalitarianism remains fundamentally detrimental to individual liberties. The Bundeswehr prioritizes the value of freedom.

Leadership, characterized by a contemporary approach that emphasizes bottom-up initiatives. Historically, this phenomenon was referred to as a grassroots movement. The entirety of the book demonstrates that this approach would impose excessive demands on the individual, as Inner Leadership represents a genuine manifestation of leadership that necessitates the acquisition of suitable information, aptitude, and experience (i.e., the ability of judgment).

[118] Op. cit. von Baudissin.p. 290

4.3   Third Axiom

Prioritizing your life - **Contrasts in leadership arise from the necessity of personal life reality.** - *Fundamentals of Character*

After looking at society and the prevailing spirit as well as the timeless value of freedom, the attention shifts to the individual soldier, who is not to be viewed as a tool to serve as a means, but to make him to keep in mind "always also as an end in itself." This formulation, which appears once more in Kant, necessitates clarification.

The shorter the word, the more likely it is that it will be skipped or overlooked when reading Kant. However, they are the true decoder of the meaning. The grammatical filler words "always also" in our quotation fulfill this role since they signify an ever-present overlap between many concepts. This is the case, but there is *always also* something more to consider as well. But first, the complete quotation, which basically covers the entire Enlightenment picture of man in one statement and is required for a democratic state and its armed forces, i.e., can establish an axiom. "For rational beings are all subject to the law that each of them should never treat itself and all others merely as a means, but at the same time as an end in itself."[119] Kant presents two self-purpose formulations in his work, both of which prioritize the individual.

Kant's primary focus lies not on the potential exploitation of others, where an individual is coerced into serving someone else's objectives, but rather on the intriguing prospect of self-exploitation, when one willingly sacrifices oneself as a mere instrument to attain certain ends. This also has implications for the golden rule (treat others as you would like to be treated), as it lacks mechanisms that are self-destructive or pose a threat to one's self-esteem. The act of self-exploitation, such as engaging in behaviors that harm one's physical well-being or undermine one's self-esteem, can be considered a violation of the principles of human dignity. It remains imperative for individuals to maintain self-reflection and introspection.

Naturally, the inclusion of "all others" is also evident, demonstrating a discerning perspective. Treating others as a means aligns with the prevailing human conception of the Enlightenment (e.g.: The bus driver, with whom I board the bus, serves as a necessary intermediary in order for me to reach my desired location.) Similar to the case of a soldier who is given a directive and is obligated to execute it, the focus lies not on his personal opinions, pleasures, and concerns, but rather on his assigned tasks. No obstacles hinder the

---

[119] Immanuel Kant, „Grundlegung zur Metaphysik der Sitten (1781)", *Akademieausgabe AA Bd IV*, 1907, p-.433.Kant designates the individual as the rational being, employing a language that is free from gender-specific connotations. This approach inadvertently challenges the prevalent bias that philosophy is predominantly produced by and for males.

attainment of this perspective, and the individual in a position of authority is not obligated to imitate the exaggerated portrayal of a social educator. The supervisor can communicate their desires and expectations.

It is at this juncture that the previously described concept of "always also" becomes relevant, expanding the perspective and focusing it on the tasked individual. The specific appearance of this matter is totally delegated to the acuity and accuracy of the superior's faculty of discernment. The appropriateness of the tone of address, a gesture, a few personal sentences preceding the issuance of an order, or any other factor is determined by the *distinctiveness of the situation*. This must be appropriately molded by a knowledgeable, experienced, articulate, and compassionate figure of authority. It is imperative that the superior maintains the ability to *directly observe* and engage with their comrades and soldiers. The act of being observed holds significant value and individuals are cognizant of whether they are acknowledged or disregarded. There is a proliferation of various manifestations of disdain. The efficacy of communication is not contingent solely upon its linguistic formulation and polish; rather, the aim and attitude of the superior inevitably become discernible over an extended period. - An examination of the grievances submitted and pending for resolution reveals that most challenges encountered by soldiers stem from a lack of visibility to their superior. Once a sense of mutual distrust has been established, individuals actively seek out and identify occurrences that serve as evidence to substantiate this prevailing discomfort. This phenomenon undermines preparedness for action and should not be dismissed as inconsequential only based on this rationale. The accessibility of a superior is crucial in the implementation of Inner Leadership, which *always also* contributes to a state of constant readiness for action.

The concept of the "always also" as a perpetual coexistence of diverse elements can be observed in the works of Schiller[120], who constructs his aesthetics upon this principle. Regarding the significance of aesthetics as a fundamental aspect of Inner Leadership, the proposition of its importance, devoid of any other argument, appears audacious. The resolution in this context, akin to the concept of "contemporary," resides in a discernible shift in the semantic interpretation of the term. In contemporary discourse, the concept of aesthetics has predominantly come to be associated with artistic design. However, the philosophical perspective of the 18th century has a significantly larger understanding of this term. Ultimately, the concept pertains to the interplay between contrasting elements, which is a ubiquitous characteristic of individuals' lived experiences. The domain of aesthetics encompasses the relationship between the individual and society, as well as the

---

[120] Cf. ch. 3.2

individual and the collective. The inclusion of beauty as a contributing factor in this context serves as an additional source of motivation. Schiller's description of the cosmopolitan adeptly integrates the concerns of both individuals and the collective, allowing for harmonious integration into society without sacrificing one's distinct identity.

The Inner Leadership framework elucidates that it is incumbent upon the superior to possess a comprehensive understanding of the intricate nature of personal objectives and obligations, emotions and cognitive faculties, individual motivation and responsibilities. This understanding facilitates the development of profound insights and subsequent actions that are applicable to all, while *always also* simultaneously considering the unique needs and circumstances of everyone. The democratic and aesthetic objectives exhibit a close relationship, to the extent that they can be considered almost synonymous. In order to maintain its integrity and prioritize individual welfare, democracy ought to incorporate aesthetic considerations.

What does that signify in tangible or specific expressions? In many instances, individuals often face constraints that limit the amount of time available for deliberate and thoughtful decision-making. However, this circumstance is not inherently sad, as experienced and contemplative individuals tend to cultivate an *internal disposition* that leads to a degree of automatism.[121] The execution of actions is predominantly carried out without conscious awareness, although it is theoretically possible to provide justification with sufficient deliberation. The distinction between *unconscious action* and *mere handling* lies in the fact that the latter lacks comprehension of its activities and, at most, operates based on a trial-and-error approach rather than logical reasoning. The individual in a position of authority, characterized by a resolute demeanor, demonstrates a high level of expertise in their subconscious behaviors. Individuals who do not possess this quality are left with only fewer desirable characteristics. Democratic leaders are deemed undesirable when they possess a tendency to engage in intellectually simplistic thinking, as perceived by their subordinates.

There is a need for a reexamination of the founding fathers of Inner Leadership. The professional leader is distinguished by behaviors that are frequently unconscious, yet if given ample time, would survive critical analysis. From this experience, an individual cultivates a mindset that embodies the qualities of an effective leader, a perception that is shared by others. Eberhard Wagemann asserts that the primary objective of a superior, as exemplified by Ulrich de Maizière, is to persuade others through their personal qualities: "The

---

[121] Cf. Thomas Wanninger, *Bildung und Gemeinsinn: Ein Beitrag zur Pädagogik der Urteilskraft aus der Philosophie des „sensus communis"* (Bayreuth: Bayreuth Univ. Diss, 1999), pp. 107 ff.

forces and values that had shaped the democratic constitution, the will to freedom and shared responsibility, they must also determine service in the armed forces. Count Baudissin, as a pragmatist, demanded the same. But de Maizière recognized that education in co-responsibility is a long, never-ending process, less a question of command and obedience, more the task of convincing by *example*.[122]"

The example provided pertains solely to leadership behavior that is direct and commonplace in nature. In previous eras, the process described here would have been referred to as "shaping" the soldier. However, it is important to note that this phrase is inadequate since it fails to adequately highlight the essential self-engagement of the soldier, which is crucial for fostering a sense of shared responsibility. The concept of values and freedom is a topic of significant academic interest. The prerequisite for every member of a democratic armed force is the *intrinsic desire* to engage in specific actions and the proper conduct of oneself properly. In the end, anything can be ordered and commanded, but it goes without saying that someone else must desire it. Hence, it is imperative to have two essential conditions in place: firstly, an individual who sets the example, and secondly, another individual who not only replicates the example, but also possesses the desire to comprehend the fundamental essence of the example, specifically the attitude and insight that it embodies. Moreover, this individual should possess the intellectual capacity to engage in such an endeavor. "Inner leadership is not merely a compilation of prescriptive guidelines or formulas.[123]"

The term "example," which has persisted in both English and Romance languages, places great emphasis on the significance of its meaning. The Latin verb *eximere*, which can be most accurately rendered as "picked out, selected," denotes the act of making a *decision from a multitude of potential options*. There exist multiple potential courses of action; however, what distinguishes one as appropriate and meaningful while rendering the other unsuitable? This example extends its focus beyond the practical demonstration and instead concentrates its attention onto the selection process. In order to achieve success in the realm of Inner Leadership, four essential elements must be present. *Fundamental principles* (axioms) consistently pertain to the process of choosing and possess inherent comprehensibility without requiring additional argumentation. Furthermore, it is imperative for leadership to possess *expertise*, as it is essential for them to comprehend the military significance and purpose. The leadership process is contingent upon a military substance, since the form (i.e., the manner in which leadership is executed) necessitates the

---

122 Wagemann, *Fortwirkende Impulse für die „Innere Führung"*, pp.116f..
123 Op. cit. Wagemann.p. 117.

presence of substantive content (i.e., the specific elements that constitute leadership) for its existence. Moreover, it is essential to emphasize the significance of *practice* in mastering complex concepts. It is evident that such mastery cannot be achieved instantaneously, therefore requiring no additional explanation. Lastly, it requires a level of overall *cognitive ability*. I hold a personal preference for this particular terminology over the concept of intelligence. One perspective to consider is that psychology has assumed authority over various domains of "intelligence," while another perspective emphasizes the importance of clear discernment in making sound judgments. The establishment of a distinct boundary, particularly inside the military domain, holds significant importance. The utilization of vague expressions and broad generalizations does not contribute to the effective decision-making process in specific instances. In this context, it is essential that the *message is characterized by clarity and distinctness*. However, it is important to note that the address should be preceded by a thorough evaluation of leadership performance through focused selection.

The ability of a superior to effectively fulfill this exemplary role is contingent upon their experience as a cohesive individual, enabling them to adeptly reconcile and integrate contradictory elements. The concept of Inner Leadership does not entail the soldier assuming a facade to blend in and conform to societal norms[124], so presenting a stark contrast to their true self. In their maturity, they are the representative of both militancy and civility. According to Wolf von Baudissin, the disciplinary superior plays a crucial role in this context, as various aspects of military and sometimes personal life intersect with their authority. According to Schiller, the cosmopolitan can be understood as the individual who serves as the central figure, exerting a significant influence on the overall environment. "The human center, whose charisma decisively determines the atmosphere. Without a certain amount of - I would like to say - free enthusiasm, knowledge and skills, they will not be able to meet the many demands placed on them in the everyday life of peace. If we now project their task onto times of tension or even onto the battlefield, it becomes clear what a burden lies on these people. (...) But the most important thing is that the most important part of leadership cannot be read from the duty roster. It takes place in all types of training (... and) in the conversation during an exercise break. The climate in which duty and free time take place is of crucial importance. It can clarify the values to be defended, convey the feeling of partnership and thus create a firm and resilient foundation from which everything else follows almost by itself. [125] " Baudissin also

---

[124] op. cit. Wagemann, p.113.
[125] von Baudissin, *Grundwert Frieden*, p.291.

acknowledges the concept, but he considers not just the positive influence of a competent disciplinary superior, but also the negative influence of an inappropriate one, where circumstances can potentially result in a complete reversal of expected outcomes.[126]

If an individual engages in critical thinking beyond the immediate context and disregards the aforementioned third principle, the soldier may lose sight of their superior, so jeopardizing the entire situation. If core values are not acquired within the unit, what principles should be safeguarded? To what extent does the operational effectiveness of a company suffer when the unit commander lacks genuine interest and commitment towards the soldiers under their command?

To ensure the soldier remains in the forefront of our thoughts, it is necessary to include a final quotation that was evidently deliberated upon by Baudissin, de Maizière, and von Kielmansegg, thereby rendering it of exceptional significance. Furthermore, it captures the artistic conflict between emotion and rationality, as elucidated by Schiller, that advocates for a harmonious synthesis. Kant's ideas are also cited, however expressed in a somewhat rigid manner. *Therefore, it can be argued that the following statement is of significant importance, as it highlights the alignment between the new Inner Leadership of the Axioms and the preexisting doctrine:* "The question of the image of man also includes the much-discussed problem of whether the soldier should preferably be approached via *emotion* or via *ratio*. We concluded that conscious manipulation of the emotional world is inhumane and, moreover, leads to nihilism, skepticism and rebellion as soon as the intention is recognized. We think that democracy, the modern world of work and the soldier's craft demand rational action and that only the soldier who feels challenged by his task faces up to it, and that as an individual, i.e. undivided with his intellect, feeling and ability. This is especially true when he feels that he is not being addressed as a means to an end, but with respect for his dignity. A consistent and convincingly pursued education brings imperceptible but all the more profound experiences, impressions and insights.[127]"

---

[126] op. cit.
[127] Op. cit. pp. von Baudissin, *Grundwert Frieden*, pp.293ff.

4.4 Fourth Axiom

Keeping your ideals in mind - the Condition of Democracy and the Military Mission define and complement each other. - *Principle of Complementarity*

Habits of cognition exhibit a prolonged duration. The initial impression of this aphorism may be deemed nonsensical at initial examination, and potentially under more scrutiny as well. Undoubtedly, the matter is addressed by the field of systematics. Nevertheless, it is consistently remarkable that the concept of opposition is seen crucial for discerning the true significance. Furthermore, the absence of opposing concepts renders the desired outcome indescribable and hence incapable of being conceptualized.

The subsequent discussion briefly returns to Hegel. Hegel employed a novel linguistic framework to express the notion that the absolute embodies the simultaneous coexistence of identity and non-identity, encompassing both opposition and unity: **"The absolute itself, however, is therefore the identity of identity and non-identity; opposition and oneness are in it at the same time."**[128] The section from the *Differenzschrift*, frequently cited in the scientific community, is notable for its apparent contradiction. In any case, the typical response is to determine whether something is identical or not. An object or concept can be categorized as either hot or cold, acceptable or unsuitable, democratic or undemocratic, freedom-granting or constraining, but it cannot possess both qualities simultaneously. This statement encapsulates Hegel's concept of identity and non-identity.

In order to enhance comprehensibility, we will employ a line of reasoning that has already been articulated in a comparable manner within the framework of the systematics of Inner Leadership. The initial stage involves the *recognition of one's identity through the process of self-comparison with others*. It is recommended to rephrase this sentence in a manner that highlights the fundamental alignment of one's thinking with that of Hegel. The second step involves the recognition of one's own identity through the process of self-comparison with individuals who are not oneself: Who **I** am myself, I can only recognize when I see **ME** in comparison to others (**not-me**). From a mathematical perspective, it is possible to express the concept as follows: I = ME + non-me. This statement elucidates Hegel's concept of the relationship between identity and non-identity.

What is the significance of this? The perception of a democratic armed force is often regarded as contradictory. It is purported that the Bundeswehr and NATO espouse a commitment to peace and freedom. However, their actions appear to contradict this stance, since they engage in the acquisition of

---

[128] Hegel, *Differenz des Fichteschen und Schellingschen Systems (kurz: Differenzschrift)*, p.85.

84

weaponry for warfare while potentially neglecting or limiting the rights of citizens in the process. Another example can be observed when engaging in conversations with former conscripts who fulfilled their military service out of a genuine obligation rather than a mere sense of duty, and who maintained a reserved disposition towards the Bundeswehr. It is frequently reported that these individuals experienced a perplexing environment within the Bundeswehr, characterized by a multitude of contradictions that lacked clear purpose or meaning to them.

However, what is the rationale behind justifying *the requirement of contradictions?* For certain individuals, the pragmatic aspect of having access to the fire department as a means of preparedness for any unforeseen circumstances, and the necessity of training for such scenarios, may be satisfactory. Another individual prefers to mention the Roman philosopher Cicero and his famous quote: "*Si vis pacem para bellum.*" The adage "_Whom wants peace prepares for war" suggests that taking proactive measures to ensure military strength and readiness might serve as a deterrent to potential adversaries, hence promoting a more peaceful environment. Adhering to the idea of prioritizing possession over necessity, there exists a perception of assurance in possessing a readily available force, even in the absence of immediate requirement.

However, it should be noted that these practical arguments do not serve as a scientific justification for the impositions associated with the armed forces. If this book aims to give a notion of Inner Leadership that goes beyond a mere compilation of practical concerns, it is imperative to seek an alternative explanation. Upon examining Hegel's work, this becomes readily apparent.

Democracy inherently revolves around the adherence to democratic principles, wherein a significant number of individuals perceive these principles as personally valuable and aspire to embody them in their own lives. The challenging quotation from Hegel will now be addressed once more, albeit with a different emphasis. Hegel states: "The **Absolute itself**, however, is therefore the identity of identity and non-identity; opposition and oneness are in it at the same time." Translated in the context of justice, this implies that the presence of experiences involving both justice and injustice is essential for an individual to embrace justice as a personal value. Hegel designates the notion of "justice," which emerges in individuals via the encounter of complementary opposites, as the "absolute." Plato, on the other hand, would have referred to it as an "idea." This concept can readily be extended to analogous democratic principles such as dignity, liberty, egalitarianism, and respect. The concept of the absolute refers to the ideal or embodiment of justice, devoid of any specific considerations, intentions, or practical execution. In contemporary computer science, the term "absolute" refers to the hardware component of a computer system. This component, while lacking autonomous functionality, is essential for the operation of the software, which encompasses the tangible applications and programs.

Consequently, in order to cultivate a democratic ethos, it is important to possess familiarity with both democratic principles *and* their antitheses. When a soldier experiences a temporary restriction in their freedom, or when a superior imposes such restrictions on their subordinates, it can be argued that this does not constitute a violation of freedom. Instead, he explicitly affirms this notion as the pursuit of freedom in the presence of potential and real dangers remains the primary objective. It is incumbent upon individuals in positions of authority to elucidate this matter. The Inner Leadership of the Bundeswehr has always expressed opposition towards the notion of hardship as a standalone objective or as a kind of harassment. The imposition of hardship and limitations on freedom has practical purposes in the acquisition of military skills and the cultivation of endurance. Additionally, it facilitates a deeper understanding of the concept of freedom. The process of oscillation between value and non-value, aimed at cultivating a comprehensive understanding of own values, is a fundamental aspect of the Inner Leadership framework. The concept of "spiritual armor," as previously discussed within this book, further emphasizes this process. It may be argued that this oscillating process serves as a platform for the cultivation and promotion of democratic principles.

This technique is also reflective of common experiences and real-life circumstances. For instance, in order to underscore the significance of peace, it is imperative to juxtapose it with the concept of war. The latter may be traced back to its origins with Heraclitus, whom Hegel explicitly acknowledges as a source of inspiration. Heraclitus, in his Fragments, consistently presents opposing elements as a unified whole, a theme that Hegel finds particularly noteworthy. "One part of a pair of opposites never appears completely independently but is always conditioned by the other part of the pair of opposites. [129]" The duty of comprehending the distinguishing and unifying aspects, even within a complex circumstance, is attributed to the faculty of understanding (*logos*) according to Heraclitus. In his discourse, logos is occasionally employed interchangeably with the soul (*psyche*), and at times, with fire and lightning. Undoubtedly, a profound comprehension permeates the entirety of the human being and engulfs them, like to the intensity of fire, particularly when pertaining to matters of significance and value. In the process, the realization, for which one must occasionally wait a long time in a sultry state of mind, abruptly appears. It illuminates everything from one moment to the next, the

---

[129] Christof Rapp, *Vorstokratiker* (München: C. H. BECK, 1997), p.84.

(complex) world has changed, and despite contradictions, there is a solution.[130]

This argument serves as the foundation for a genuine understanding of Inner Leadership within the humanities, making it an axiom that is evident even prior to the commencement of any tangible value creation. Furthermore, it is supported by practical experience. An individual in the developmental stage of childhood or adolescence, who is solely granted freedoms without any corresponding responsibilities or limitations, may fail to fully comprehend or value the significance and importance of such freedoms. Individuals who have been indulged excessively tend to develop an insatiable need for further gratification. However, this insatiable pursuit eventually encounters constraints, leading to the formation of an internal perception of freedom. This perception arises from the realization that every act of free will inherently involves the establishment of boundaries, encompassing both affirmative and negative aspects. During childhood, individuals often make choices to engage in a particular game, so excluding themselves from participating in other games for a specific period. Similarly, as young adults, individuals make decisions to pursue a specific job, thereby forgoing the opportunity to acquire knowledge and skills in alternative vocations.

The bestowal of liberty, as well as the establishment of boundaries and constraints, can be regarded as a kind offering. Education provides individuals with a profound understanding of freedom and other intrinsic values, which cannot be *rationally* constructed through alternative means.[131] Individuals who want to discourage a misinterpretation of the concept of freedom inadvertently harm both the individual and the community. This is because the absence of restrictions alone does not give birth to a comprehensive understanding of freedom at the individual level.[132]

Individuals who fail to appreciate the significance of liberty are prone to being oblivious to the tangible absence of freedom and the resultant ramifications. This also poses a persistent *threat to democracy originating from its own internal dynamics*. Individuals who possess limited knowledge solely about

---

[130] This is also how the fragment 64 "Das Weltall aber steuert der Blitz" (The universe, however, is controlled by lightning), much admired by Hans-Georg Gadamer and Martin Heidegger, is to be understood.

[131] The topic of freedom education by setting limits was first mentioned by J.J. Rousseau in his educational novel " Emil – Oder über die Erziehung" (Emil - Or About Education). This book had a demonstrable influence on Immanuel Kant and the entire Age of Enlightenment.

[132] The concept of health holds a similar level of importance. Individuals lacking an understanding of the concept of illness are unable to appreciate the significance of good health. Furthermore, the inevitable temporal constraint imposed by mortality, sometimes referred to as death, serves to underscore the worth of time.

favorable experiences and advantageous aspects tend to overlook the potential dangers associated with such circumstances. The reason for their inability to see them is not due to a lack of desire, but rather due to an inner constraint. The conceptualization of freedom presented lacks adequate development and is inherently limited in its potential for further elaboration. This significant inference derived from the philosophical perspectives of Hegel and Heraclitus.

The intricate relationship between freedom, individual dignity, and the necessary constraints on freedom to uphold a free society and effectively safeguard it during times of necessity has consistently been a focal point in the study of Inner Leadership. This analysis focuses on the early establishment of the Bundeswehr and its objective to develop the concept of Inner Leadership. Eberhard Wagemann, who references Ulrich de Maizière, says: "The objective was to find a balance between traditional soldierly values and contemporary circumstances. A soldierly order had to be implemented, which begins with the concept of civic rights and responsibilities, seeks compliance and obedience based on insight and consent, but also adds the amount of compulsion - and command is compulsion - that the soldierly task requires if insight is insufficient or absent. The citizen in uniform is not meant to be "soft," but "hard," perhaps harsher than ever before; but hardened through meaningful training, oriented to the gravity of the demands of war, which respects the individual's personal honor and dignity.[133]"

There would be much more evidence to support the notion that Inner Leadership consistently prioritizes obedience stemming from deep understanding. An endeavor was made to substantiate a potential true insight by drawing upon the philosophical framework of Hegel. The concept can be succinctly summarized as the notion that democratic values emerge solely via the dynamic interaction of contrasting elements. This statement suggests that it is logically imperative to consider various perspectives in order to develop a comprehensive understanding, since failing to do so would hinder the formation of an individual's subjective evaluation and significance. However, this understanding does not imply that every experience must be personally encountered. The notion of incarceration alone is often adequate for an intellectually average individual to form a decisive aversion against a life characterized by imprisonment.

To mitigate such misinterpretations, it is important to clarify that the concept of complementarity generates value through the absence of opposing elements rather than their simultaneous existence. The concept of *identity and*

---

[133] Maizière, U. de quoted by: Wagemann, *Fortwirkende Impulse für die „Innere Führung“*, p.118. Zum Handeln aus Einsicht, see also von Baudissin, *Grundwert Frieden*, p.289.

non-identity as posited by Hegel signifies a state of unity, albeit not one that occurs simultaneously. Primarily, it should be noted that the existence of contradictions does not imply that they would be reconciled by a universal homogeneity. In relation to Heraclitus, who is present throughout this book and whose influence can also be observed in its subsequent growth, it may be asserted that "interactions between opposites (are) a natural process necessary for the continuation of the world we know.[134]" Thereby, no opposition should continuously dominate, but a balance or a constant measure must be maintained.

The establishment of a suitable correlation between complementary opposites does not imply absolute equality, but rather acknowledges the distinct existence and rationale of each. To effectively navigate the complexities of contradictory information on the internet, it is imperative to possess an always alert intellect (*logos*). This entails more than just factual knowledge, but also encompasses the profound process of internalization, heartfelt engagement, experiential understanding, and even personal tribulations. Today, it is plausible to refer to this phenomenon as the convergence of cognitive and affective aptitude.

These values, which are acquired in various aspects of service and life, possess inherent worth and provide individuals with the opportunity to cultivate a resilient mindset throughout time. The formation of values necessitates the presence of difficulties and the process of critically engaging with opposing perspectives. Wagemann again cites de Maizière: "Peace is secured 'by a high standard of training, equipment and the inner attitude of all soldiers every day'. For de Maizière, there is 'no contradiction between peacekeeping and combat readiness.[135]"

The juxtaposition of combat preparation and peacekeeping as an "*irrevocable paradoxia of military service*" is intriguing, particularly when considering the preceding quotation on the inner attitude. This cannot be allowed to remain unchanged. The crucial element has been disregarded. This book explores the various questions surrounding identity, the democratic ideal, and the potential for value formation derived from it. It takes a significant leap forward by incorporating Hegel's concept of the absolute. The focus lies not on *the paradox inside the soldier's occupation*, but rather on the *parallelism* between one's *experiences and thoughts*. It is via this complimentary contrast that one's true intentions and democratic beliefs become evident.

---

[134] Rapp, *Vorstokratiker*, p.84.
[135] Op. cit. Rapp,.p 122.

4.5   Fifth Axiom

With you in mind -Democracy is protected as a means of establishing one's own unique personality. - *Principle of Identity*

The fact that we humans are beings who are oriented towards community which also results in responsibility for others, is a commonplace. However, the *other's identity* has greater meaning. This "more" is qualitative rather than quantitative, which makes it difficult to comprehend, as "more" does not exist in "other"-focused reasoning. A true community is marked by *respect* and *mindfulness*, as well as by *respect* and *decency* for all members. Remembering our *humanity, tolerance*, and *core values* is essential. This is not to say that these ideas do not have important connections to community in a defended state, but all they do is create a link, an intersection, between people, which has nothing to do with who they are as individuals.

In general, the concepts around the word 'community' serve to separate the "me" from the "others". This is a customary practice in our society. We have had several decades of time to specialize or diversify. The musicians "Adventure with Kess" features the lyric, "I am me and you are you" for kids. Although the importance of working together to get things done is discussed, each reference also emphasizes the uniqueness of each person, which is viewed as educationally useful by many.

The principle of 'respect' acts the same way because, above all else, uniqueness is valued. This describes one method to a *modus vivendi*, one that each party can tailor to their own preferences. Essentially, respect and tolerance do not create community. They place a premium on diversity and individuality, stressing that people should value their differences more than their similarities with others and learning to live with viewpoints and approaches to life that are starkly at odds with their own. A different sort of community, one that does not stress the limits of individuality but rather builds identity, must therefore apply to the soldier who is depending on comradeship and the combat community. Therefore, a different form of community must be established for the Inner Leadership of a democratic military force, one that is distinct from the typical togetherness seen in other contexts.

Even though religious confession has declined and the state, consciously defines itself laicistically, like in France for example, the form of thought with the individual at its center has remained unchanged in the West, and this can be traced back to the religious tradition.

On one hand, the idea of "selection" provides a striking example of religious individualism. Christianity is all about the individual, but Judaism emphasizes the selected people (a "group individuality") that nevertheless recognizes the chosen person (freedom fighters, kings, and prophets). At his baptism, he is called by name, given an assignment, and given the expectation of a personal resurrection. The emphasis on the individual is apparent, and it is not challenged by philosophical thought from the Renaissance forward at the earliest, or the modern period at the latest.

Conversely, the delineation between the individual and society, as well as the distinction between oneself and others, becomes indistinct when one recognizes that we *coexist not in isolation, but in a state of interconnectedness*. The pronoun "I" is a unique entity that solely identifies itself in this manner.

Emanuel Levinas adopts a completely Hegelian way of thinking. The deliberate inclusion of the emphasis on uniqueness in the fourth axiom is intended to prepare the mind for a novel and original viewpoint. The presence of one is contingent upon the presence of the other. To put it in more philosophical terms, there is an ontological community—that is, a *shared existence in the self and the other*—between me and the other. Furthermore, this demonstrates why the terms "community" and "connection" are overly nebulous. It is more accurate to refer to what Emanuel Levinas calls "chaining" and "hostage of the other".

Now is a good time to circle back to the Inner Leadership systems that was mentioned briefly before: Through one another, we each come into our own unique selves. This is most evident in the case of a young infant, who would not only fail to develop into a self-confident personality but would also perish if nobody cared emotionally and made another I recognized.[136]

Why should soldiers care about these ideas, which can be traced all the way back to Levinas? In typical daily duties, treating each other as equals may be all that's required. That is not sufficient for combat and war. The decisions made by superiors, shared knowledge, and camaraderie are crucial to everyone's survival. If one is willing to make the mental leap, one might compare the battle community to the early stages of existence, when there is an existential dependency, a "chaining" with the other, without whom one cannot survive in conflict and cannot complete the task.

It's possible to relate the lyrics of "The good Comrade" to this situation. Specifically, "He lies at my feet, as if it were a piece of me." Today's generation, raised in relative tranquilly, has little chance of understanding the full importance of this. However, the text's seeming simplicity belies the complexity of the soldier's existence and the inseparability of killing and death from his line of work. And the shared conviction that we can make it through this; if my friend doesn't, a little bit of me dies with him.

---

136 Cf. the answers to the key questions at the end of section 3.4.

In a battle, one's own survival is contingent on the actions of others. Maybe there's nothing wrong with the tried-and-true, civilian-tested dichotomy of "me" and "the other" in terms of esteem, respect, and reciprocal complementation. It is no longer adequate in the context of the soldier's job for two main reasons:

1.   Momentarily, the *camaraderie* dissolves the individuality. The limits of identity are brought into sharp focus in reports, writings, and films about war and deployment. This existential need to carry on alive only functions in the rare circumstance where there is little to no discernible difference between equals. This bond is partially lived into the trauma through death and wounds. The "eye of the hurricane," not some philosophical side matter. A spiritual bond is maintained, especially to the departed comrades, long after battle and deployment have ended. How many veterans have spent their entire lives mourning their fallen friends, even after going home to their families?

The conclusion is supported by analysis of the Bundeswehr's deployment history. The tremendous physical and psychological pressures of soldiers on deployment are depicted in all of them, as summed up by Uwe Hartmann: "What they all have in common is the description of the high physical and psychological stresses on soldiers during deployment. Many openly address the fact that they suffered from exhaustion and were no longer fully operational at times. They agree that the craft of arms must be mastered, that it is a matter of being able to fight and wanting to fight if need be. This is also a direct consequence of *camaraderie*. Everyone must be able to rely on each other. Everyone emphasizes that they were often lucky, that mistakes always happen had to be quickly ironed out by others so that no bad consequences occurred. These are all aspects that belong to the good soldier.[137]" For our purposes, the so-called "ironing out of mistakes" is crucial because, at its core, it simply means that a soldier assumes the identity of the other and performs, under pressure, tasks that the other is now unable to complete. In this situation, people put aside their differences to work together for the greater good of saving lives and completing the goal.

2.   Another way in which the blurring of "me" and "not-me (other)" is important for the soldier is in the context of the soldier's heroic efforts to protect the rights and liberties of the German population.

It's not enough to put forth effort and resources in the name of national *defense*. The business owner relies on what is fleeting and fungible, whereas the soldier risks what is both *permanent and irreplaceable*: his life. This is what

---

[137] Hartmann, *Der gute Soldat. Politische Kultur und soldatisches Selbstverständnis heute*, pp.141f.

sets the soldier apart from the physician, educator, politician, and healthcare provider. True, they all sacrifice decades of their lives for the common good, but nobody gives up their very existence. Another qualitative distinction that cannot be described by connection, esteem, and respect is the willingness to risk one's health and one's life for the other, who in this case is worth at least as much to me as I am to myself.

Baudissin explains that "Only a good citizen can recognize military service as part of his civic responsibility; only *he knows and feels* what is at stake. This is the goal of Inner Leadership. It achieves this goal by training and guiding the soldier in such a way that his critical mind and alert conscience enable him to think, act responsibly and independently. (...) This demand does not only result from the truism that democracy does not stop at the barracks gate, but also from the realization that units with soldiers of a different attitude fall apart in today's combat.[138]"

This citation lends itself to numerous fruitful readings. What matters, however, is that Baudissin considers the military profession thoroughly. Falling apart in warfare should be avoided at all costs. Fear of a superior by a regular soldier may have worked in the past, but it has no place in a modern, democratic society. There is no military value without the desired unity and military goal.

Arguments are necessary for making headway in a speech or a book, but Baudissin also refers to emotion. It centers on the soldier who has a personal understanding of the stakes. Trust, confidence, and a sense of safety stemming from knowing one's own family and close friends are also a part of one's comradeship unit.

The fifth axiom analyzes the *emotion* in detail. True love is the foundation for unity, and without unity, no task can be completed.

---

[138] von Baudissin, *Grundwert Frieden*, p.298.

5. Opportunities for Inner Leadership - An Outlook

The five axioms have been revisited considering additional elements and the acknowledgment of the founding fathers of Inner Leadership, building upon the previous explorations and methodical framework. The existing text already furnishes a summary, rendering the inclusion of additional summarizing information somewhat redundant at this juncture.

What remains pertinent, however, is a conclusive examination that definitively delves into the inquiry that has already assumed a significant role in the introductory section, specifically the potential for Inner Leadership to articulate a *critique* of itself. In this instance, the *three narrative strands* of the novel are once again examined in a concise manner.

1. *The influence of Inner Leadership can take effect when an individual's soul comprehends.* The focus of this discussion pertains to the faculty of judgment, as previously alluded to in the introductory citation attributed to Heraclitus: "Bad witnesses are people's eyes and ears when the soul does not understand their language."

Heraclitus, a pre-Socratic philosopher, adopts a methodology akin to that of Hegel, wherein oscillation -the weighing, are significant components play a vital role. Clausewitz exhibited comparable behavior. The sensory organs alone provide a perception that lacks interpretation. The concept of the soul, which is believed to be the source of life and the center of cognitive processes, provides access to the understanding of reality.[139] There exists no singular regulation that only pertains to cognitive faculties and can engender a holistic comprehension. The imposition of rules alone results in a lack of vitality and dynamism. The exclusion of prior Inner Leadership from the lives of the troops is an unavoidable consequence since it isolates itself from reality by adhering rigidly to rules and relying on clichéd statements. Watzlawick's discourse on digital and analogue communication encompassed the subject matter at hand. The range of potential interpretations for comprehending a given circumstance is exceedingly vast. The complete instruction of these methods cannot be imparted by any individual; rather, the student must acquire understanding via personal exploration. Examples can serve as a catalyst for developing intuition and comprehension. Nevertheless, it should be noted that relying solely on learning from examples, also known as best practice, does not guarantee confidence in one's action. This is mostly due to the fact that there is an infinite number of potential scenarios that might arise in reality, making it impossible to have an exhaustive collection of case descriptions that encompass all possible situations. Example, reflection, and practice are three methods of comprehension. Schiller's

---

[139] Cf. Hans-Georg Gadamer, *Der Anfang der Philosophie* (Stuttgart: Reclam, 1996), pp.77f.

cosmopolitan is characterized as a someone who possesses a well-rounded education, enabling them to make informed and suitable decisions in specific situations. In this context, Schiller also discusses the concept of genius. There is a certain level of ingenuity associated with the ability to locate the appropriate item at the precise moment and in the suitable manner, to articulate it in a way that is easily understood, and eventually executed. The impact of a military order, which provides manual instructions, on this situation is negligible. In the most unfavorable scenario, it engenders a misguided perception of safety. Regulations do not have the power to deprive superiors of their capacity for cognitive and behavioral functioning.

Navigating a personal, professional, and political context, particularly when occupying a position of authority within the Bundeswehr, presents considerable challenges due to the convergence of numerous aspects. Hence, it is reasonable to employ the term "soul" rather than solely relying on limited *insights* in certain domains, as the latter would be insufficient. The entirety encompasses not only the acquisition of knowledge but also the *personal sentiment* and the *engagement* with others as distinct individuals. Furthermore, an additional element is introduced, which encompasses both understanding and emotion. This element is known as the complementary contradiction, which exists inside the entirety of a situation and reveals the comprehensive aspects simultaneously present. To comprehend and appreciate the intricacy of this phenomenon, it is imperative to allocate sufficient time for contemplation and, ideally, allow for its gradual development. This temporal allowance is crucial for managers to possess. The reliance on impulsive action and a quick temper are frequently not advisable courses of action.

This perspective takes into consideration a military actor that possesses not only the ability to act and provide guidance, but also the capacity to contemplate and evaluate. It is evident that leaders who become engrossed in the tasks of organizing, managing, and executing are not able to effectively lead. The individuals in question have a deficiency in the intrinsic motivation required to comprehend the underlying purpose and inherent values associated with their actions, both for themselves and for others. Hans-Georg Gadamer articulates this concept in relation to the logos in Heraclitus in the following manner: "(It pertains to the) variations of a singular thought, (...) wherein the divergence, tension, opposition, sequence, and transformation constitute the sole veracity.[140]"

The concept of finding commonalities amongst opposites is a novel and unconventional approach to thinking. The extent to which natural scientific and technology advancements have impacted contemporary thought and

---

[140] Gadamer, *Der Anfang des Wissens,* p.17.

perception remains undetermined at present. However, the concept of binary code represents a very recent development in cognitive processes. The incorporation of contrasting perspectives is a characteristic of comprehensive thinking, which contrasts with traditional thinking.[141]

The comprehension of the soul and the potentiality to embody Inner Leadership is a shift from dichotomous thought patterns. For a decision to be effectively adhered to and executed, it is imperative that it is unambiguous and unequivocal. However, the pathway to achieving this goal is characterized by a wider scope, inherent contradictions, increased duration, and a greater investment of effort than initially perceived. Several prominent thinkers, including Heraclitus, Schiller, Hegel, and Levinas, have provided compelling arguments in support of this line of thought. In essence, even Immanuel Kant is affiliated with this concept, as shown in his moral philosophy through the statement of "the means to the end and *always also* of the end in itself," which establishes a unifying principle between opposing elements. The inclusion of deliberative thought as a significant factor in Clausewitz's framework suggests a potential avenue for the integration of the new Inner Leadership within the Bundeswehr.

2.   *The influence of Inner Leadership can take effect when it is based on arguments.* The objective of this study is to incorporate material that has undergone rigorous testing and, in certain instances, has been consistently cited over time. The question of determining absolute certainty in the humanities remains elusive, as it is inherently challenging to establish. However, individuals can enhance their chances of accuracy by engaging with a diverse range of literary sources. Ultimately, the effectiveness of arguments and the quality of presentation are crucial in persuading both the reader and the practitioner. These individuals will discern the author's views, expertise, and experiences, as well as their practical application, inside the written work.

The purpose of considering the axioms is to establish the fundamental basis for these arguments. Two goals are interlinked here: the presence of democratic ideals is observable on one hand, while on the other hand, their expression in axioms has become redundant in terms of argumentation.

a.   In this context, the primary emphasis is placed on society, which, in accordance with its beliefs and principles, generates a governing body that aligns with the collective ethos. The phenomenon under consideration originated within a state that was influenced by religion, and culminates with the perspectives of Böckenförde and Küng about the democratic and ethical conception of time. This conception serves as the foundation for the

---

[141] Cf. Jürgen-Eckardt Pleines, *Heraklit: Anfängliches Philosophieren (Studienbücher Antike)* (Darmstadt: Georg Olms Verlag, 2002). Jürgen Pleines also refers to Nicholas of Cues and his doctrine of the *coincidentia oppositorum*.

development of constitutions and laws, which are not self-generated but rather contingent upon external factors. This observation can also elicit feelings of fear or apprehension. At its most optimal, this sentiment serves as a source of motivation to actively engage in public service and contribute to the betterment of the state, a responsibility that individuals possess the capacity to influence to varying degrees.

Nevertheless, the interaction between society and the armed forces, which should ideally enhance and incorporate each other into the discourse, is currently in jeopardy. By adhering to the first axiom, it becomes evident that the relationship between a society and its armed forces is unidirectional, wherein the society determines the composition and characteristics of its armed forces, rather than the armed forces exerting influence over the society. The discourse in question has a unidirectional flow, wherein a reliance relationship is observed with regards to the armed forces. The values in society.

b.   The concept of timelessness can be derived from the democratic interpretation of time. Therefore, Inner Leadership can be seen as authentic leadership since it does not necessitate adaptation and remains impervious to the influence of prevailing trends or rapidly evolving circumstances, particularly within the military context. Timeless democratic Inner Leadership, therefore, rejects any kind of totalitarianism. The proponents of Inner Leadership drew inspiration from this circumstance, leading them to develop a deliberate departure from the ethos and hierarchical framework of the military. This historical era persists in the present time. The Value of Democracy.

c.   The spirit of democracy holds significant importance in the realm of political theory and government. The essence of the state and the enduring nature of democracy are inherently intertwined; nonetheless, it is important to distinguish the soldier as an individual who must personally experience and safeguard these principles during times of crisis. The superior entity enters the visual field. It is imperative for an individual to possess a comprehensive understanding of other perspectives, demonstrating a global mindset akin to Schiller's concept of being a cosmopolitan. Furthermore, one should actively engage in critical thinking, exercising sound judgment, and serving as an exemplary figure for others. The complementary elements combine to form a whole entity, and comprehension presents the potential for reciprocal comprehension from the community. The attainment of success in this endeavor cannot be guaranteed, however it remains a possibility. Fundamentals of Character.

d.   Understanding has the potential to resolve the "insoluble paradox of the soldier's profession," a challenge that de Maizière has not yet successfully addressed. Hegel employs the historical method of reconciling opposing concepts, a practice that has been recognized since ancient times. Hence, the concept of freedom and other values may emerge, deriving their significance from their inherent relationship with their corresponding antitheses. The concept of Inner Leadership is intricately linked to the traumatic experiences of World War II. It emerged as a response to the oppressive and undemocratic conditions prevailing during that time, as individuals within the Bundeswehr sought to imbue the essence of freedom into the organization. The Bundeswehr is deemed indispensable, as its absence would render its existence incomprehensible. Furthermore, empirical evidence from its initial decades of operation has demonstrated its capability to effectively execute its military objectives. The rationale for the limitation of liberties to achieve a certain objective, particularly to underscore their significance, has been elucidated. Principle of Complementarity.

e.   The comprehensive nature of Inner Leadership, encompassing all aspects of preparedness for military service, including deployment in warfare, is exemplified by the defense of democracy as a defining characteristic in the other. This facilitates the troops of the Bundeswehr to perceive themselves as members of the soldierly community, in alignment with their true identity. The individuals in question are actively engaged in a sense of camaraderie that is progressively disregarding the boundaries that separate them from others. This is because my own identity has been shaped by the influence of others, resulting in the emergence of multiple interconnected "communities." Kielmansegg employs the term "chaining" to describe the phenomenon, while Levinas refers to it as "hostage of the other". The outcome is a state of comradeship, wherein the other individual becomes an integral component of my being, and reciprocally, I become an integral component of their being. The assertion that this represents the sole viable option for collective survival in the face of lethal peril, while simultaneously ensuring the effective completion of the mission, can be deemed as very probable. Principle of Identity.

3. *The influence of Inner Leadership can take effect when all members of the armed forces perceive themselves and are perceived by others as active participants.*

The concept of the independent soldier has been a longstanding topic in the field of Inner Leadership. The utilization of "mission command" is fundamentally grounded in this principle. Nevertheless, it is necessary to consider alternative perspectives when evaluating the current perception of the Bundeswehr, as solely basing conclusions on humanistic principles may not provide a comprehensive analysis. During the process of evaluating Inner Leadership as an exemplification of potential outcomes, it is worth considering the potentialities that *could* arise and, in light of the prevailing challenges posed by warfare in Europe, the additional possibilities that *should* emerge. The focus of this discussion is not on the various methods for enhancing the

Bundeswehr, but rather on the *manner* in which Inner Leadership is exhibited in daily interactions and the effective approach to undertaking duties.

An examination of antiquity appears to hold relevance in this context, but it should not be limited by only the disciplines of history and classical philology. The foundation of ancient law rests upon three fundamental pillars: The aforementioned *principles, judgment, and privileges*.[142] This literary work also explores the concepts or axioms, and the need for exercising judgment has been a recurring topic of discussion. Consequently, the author takes a detour to delve into the historical context of the ancient forum.

The concept of *principles* aligns with the Roman interpretation of the Twelve Tables Law. The inscription was publicly engraved on the forum in a manner that transcended time, serving as the quintessential benchmark for evaluating cases in court speeches to elucidate a given circumstance.

The evaluator and speaker were required to exhibit *judgment* by effectively retracing the many aspects of the individual case to these principles and categorizing it accordingly. Alternatively, it is possible to consider the reverse approach, which involves extrapolating the underlying concept to showcase the specific situation as a representative example of the broader context. The attainment of any outcome is contingent upon the presence of perception, perspicacity, and dialectic thinking.

The concept of *privilege* can be particularly challenging to comprehend, as it has predominantly been associated with notions such as noble privilege or the advantage of the wealthy. The term has experienced an unpleasant semantic shift, resulting in a significant degradation of its societal significance and its contribution to fostering positive relationships among individuals. When it comes to practical application, which is what Roman law, like good leadership, is essentially concerned with, it is necessary to take into account contradictory principles, ambiguous allocations, or difficult circumstances. It is possible for a decision to be influenced by conflicting principles or deemed unsuitable or unethical according to a certain principle. In this scenario, it is possible to confer privileges for a specific occasion (*pro hac vice*) and to establish a distinct entitlement (*privus lex*) that supersedes the general norm.

Privileges have been observed in the historical context of the Bundeswehr, encompassing its bestowal and subsequent utilization. Troop leaders have been observed to stray from established privileges in certain justifiable individual circumstances, as evidenced by anecdotes and personal experiences, even in the face of regulations or instructions that dictate otherwise. In certain instances, this approach may be the sole method to effectively fulfill the

---

142 Wanninger, *Bildung und Gemeinsinn: Ein Beitrag zur Pädagogik der Urteilskraft aus der Philosophie des „sensus communis"*, pp.23-29.

organization's objectives while also considering the welfare of the military personnel involved. Amidst the prevailing apprehension surrounding purported instances of authority and power abuse, these individuals in positions of leadership have gone out of fashion. Nevertheless, achieving operational readiness in a military force necessitates more than just adequate equipment, supplies, and willing and capable soldiers sourced from a like-minded population. It also necessitates competent leaders who possess authority in their respective domains and are capable of effectively and actively leading.[143] The absence of financial resources and the lack of regulatory frameworks in our society, which often rely on binary modes of thought, cannot be substituted by any other means. The success of their endeavors relies on the establishment of a broad sense of trust and the overall satisfaction of their military personnel.

The erosion of leadership characterized by principles, sound judgment, and privileges over the course of several decades is not only lamentable, but also undermines the organization's operational effectiveness. As evidenced in Clausewitz's literature, the disposition of the commander towards both soldiers and troops remains consistent, encompassing a comprehensive assessment and understanding of numerous factors. The act of self-commitment driven by fear, rooted in faith in the legal system, coupled with mistrust and frustration, inevitably results in the formation of an armed force that lacks the necessary capability for effective action.

The determination of whether *Inner Leadership* has successfully produced a new narrative through its critique is subjective and dependent on individual judgment. The present endeavor has potentially resulted in a methodical categorization and rational validation of Inner Leadership, while concurrently illustrating that the majority of components necessary for a novel narrative are already encompassed inside the existing one.

A concluding remark from a personal standpoint: It is my firm belief that the preceding era of leadership within the Bundeswehr has indeed concluded. Innovations are typically generated through the establishment of new administrative domains. There appears to be a lack of concern over the genuine notion of Inner Leadership. The reorganization of existing information typically imposes significant constraints on the acquisition of new knowledge.

---

[143] It is worth noting, with due consideration to the humanistic discourse, that the troops have incurred a significant loss of decision-making autonomy as a result of the actions taken by the several federal offices of the Bundeswehr. This observation merits acknowledgment, even if it is relegated to a footnote. Although the focus of this book does not revolve around organizational reform, it is inevitable that a reconsideration of this matter is necessary. This may potentially involve the breakup of specific regions.

Inner Leadership is characterized by a lexical cohesion, since the terms used inside this model mutually elucidate one another.[144] The aforementioned system is in existence and serves to ensure the security of Inner Leadership by means of internal definition. However, it poses a significant barrier to the implementation of genuine innovations.

The current state of Inner Leadership can be characterized as a self-contained framework that derives its principles from legal-ethical and Protestant origins established before the inception of the Bundeswehr. These foundational elements are consistently reorganized and presented under several categories. There is a lack of substantial conceptual engagement.

The system's closedness is further ensured through consistent use of a singular literature as the foundational framework. The Inner Leadership framework appears to be comprised of a set of concepts that are rooted in the Basic Law or the founding fathers, with particular emphasis on the well recorded contributions of Wolf von Baudissin.[145]

What is the significance of this preoccupation with foundational principles? This can indicate that an individual is genuinely lacking advantageous circumstances and conscientiously attends to their possessions, resulting in a consistent reliance on past borrowings. The set-up and concept exhibit a limited scope. The term "concept" or "conception" refers to a collection of rules that are deemed believable within a given context, often representing a reasonable understanding or interpretation. The concept of plausibility, however, is a transitory commodity. Profound political transformations, as evidenced by historical patterns, have the potential to abruptly generate a novel state of affairs within a short span of time. The concept of Inner Leadership, which relies on plausibility, is characterized by a certain level of naivety and has the potential to become outmoded in a relatively brief period. Nevertheless, if it is grounded in the fundamental principles of democracy, it consistently exhibits forward-thinking qualities and demonstrates resilience in challenging circumstances.

What are the favorable aspects worth mentioning? The founders of Inner Leadership demonstrated a sincere commitment to Kant's imperative *sapere aude*! by employing their intellectual capacities to develop original ideas, concepts, and structures. These contributions deserve utmost admiration,

---

[144] Cf. Hans-Joachim Reeb und Peter Többicke, *Lexikon Innere Führung* (Regensburg/Berlin: Walhalla-Fachverlag, 2003).

[145] One effective method for incorporating alternative perspectives into the practice of Inner Leadership is exemplified by the work of Baran Fakir. The author makes reference to Hegel in his scholarly article titled "Dialectic of Inner Leadership" (2022). Baudissin, however, is very prevalent and appears to be primarily recognized as the sole scholar who has extensively engaged with the concept of Inner Leadership.

particularly because they were effectively implemented into practical operations and regulations, rather than remaining confined to mere noble aspirations. Nevertheless, it is still worthwhile to examine the interconnectedness and terminology of Inner Leadership in subsequent decades, with the aim of introducing novel ideas that offer alternative solutions to the existing norms. I would like to assert that there was a demand for it.

The aforementioned reference to the commencement of Inner Leadership serves to prompt an inquiry into *our overall position within the realm of Inner Leadership*. I am of the firm belief that we have yet to reach the culmination of our journey. The initial years of the Bundeswehr's Inner Leadership have resemblance to the nascent stages of philosophy in ancient Greece, akin to the era of the pre-Socratic philosophers. In addition to possessing only a *sophisticated language, dialogue partners*, and their *own cognitive faculties*, they lacked any other resources. The transmission of structured literature has been limited. The intellectuals of the ancient age demonstrated a unique understanding derived from their own insights and a thoughtful examination of human beings, the natural world, and celestial bodies.[146] This bears a striking resemblance to the initial stages of Inner Leadership, as delineated from the Himmerode memorandum onwards. It continues to stand out as an incongruous element within the prevailing military deliberations. The Wehrmacht lacked a clearly defined internal organizational structure. Prior to this instance, no individual had previously accomplished the task in the specified format. Baudissin, de Maizière and Kielmansegg are, so to speak, the pre-Socratics of Inner Leadership.

However, if one desires to pursue this line of reasoning, it becomes evident as to our current position within Inner Leadership: towards the conclusion of the initial phase. There is absolutely no justification for refraining from critically reflecting upon and considering previously established notions as unchangeable. The outcome entails the reinforcement of the administrative Inner Leadership's inherent inclination towards action. The concepts of ordering and genuine penetration have not yet been fully addressed. The concept of Inner Leadership continues to anticipate the emergence of individuals akin to Plato and Aristotle, who possess the ability to synthesize diverse perspectives into a cohesive whole.

This book aims to provide a departure from the pre-Socratic era of Inner Leadership. Furthermore, it is evident that numerous primary topics of study were not well addressed. This pertains to the inherent conflict between *safeguarding individual liberties and possessing the capability to cause widespread devastation*, which encompasses the disintegration of individuals into ashes

---

[146] Cf. Gadamer, *Der Anfang der Philosophie*, p.9-42.

instantaneously as a consequence of employing contemporary weaponry systems. - There are two other areas of conflict that warrant mention: One the one hand, it is essential to consider the inherent *personal right of every individual* and the *limitations imposed* on it, particularly in relation to the deliberate acceptance of one's own demise. On the other hand, it is crucial to examine the structure and framework of the service in question. Within this tensive environment, the individual serving as a soldier assumes the role of an *administrative* specialist who carries out their duties in a meticulous and rule-oriented fashion. However, it is important to note that he primarily identifies as a warrior, placing great significance on this role. In the realm of fencing, it is imperative for an individual to possess the ability to make sound decisions and exhibit proficiency in the art of improvisation. No victory has yet been gained with a "pencil sharpener" approach. - Furthermore, the *notion of freedom* lacks adequate elucidation. The concept of "freedom of design" is acknowledged in the book, although it is important to note that this interpretation is not exhaustive and does not encompass deterministic perspectives. The latter phenomenon had significant prominence during the 19th century, mostly due to the emergence of a natural scientific and biologistic perspective on human beings.[147]

The primary objective of these efforts is to cultivate an Inner Leadership approach that promotes a greater emphasis on humanistic thought processes. The Bundeswehr has always had a sizable representation of historians, but they are limited in their ability to assess the available data. The inquiry into the overall purpose, identification of potentialities through a critical lens, and the desire for advancement do not pertain to a historical inquiry. Furthermore, there is a lack of clarification regarding whether the initial stages of the development process include a discernible objective that can be deduced from its inception. The conclusion must be inherently present within the introduction. The culmination of a process, where one has not yet arrived, is the only point that can demonstrate the progression as a coherent and rational sequence. Therefore, the initiation itself originates from the outcome, whereby one must embark on the journey without prior knowledge of the destination. The inclusion of a hermeneutic field of tension introduces an additional dimension to the conventional inquiries within the military context.

Empirical social sciences encounter a comparable challenge since they are unable to elucidate inquiries pertaining to meaning due to their methodological orientation, which necessitates the conceptualization of the human being as an object. Jean-Paul Sartre has effectively articulated the detrimental

---

[147] Cf. op. cit. Gadamer, pp.33ff.

nature of the objective gaze. According to Sartre, when the other person is objectified and reduced to a mere subject of observation, the *mutual exchange of gazes* ceases to exist, leading to a breakdown in comprehension.[148] In the context of Inner Leadership, the significance of the gaze and the act of being observed cannot be overstated. Furthermore, there is currently no research available that assists individuals during the moment of decision-making. The ability to make accurate judgments within a decision-making context that involves time pressure, fatigue, and potential risks is mostly possessed by those with experience and a thoughtful mindset. The promotion of this mode of thinking is advocated by Inner Leadership. It is important to recall Kielmansegg's quote regarding the spear, which emphasizes the focus on the point rather than the shaft.

Both historians and empiricists, when confined within the confines of their respective disciplines, cannot deal with the future of Inner Leadership. This is due to their limited ability to solely identify and quantify existing phenomena. There are existing contexts within ordinary troop life, such as coaching, where the development of judgment as a fundamental skill for future Inner Leadership can be cultivated.

However, the potential to access the vast wealth of philosophical knowledge and insights remains untapped. Determining the underlying intention behind the limited application of humanities skills and the potential neglect of Inner Leadership remains a challenging task. There may be an additional dearth of adequately qualified employees, who, in this particular scenario, would need to join the armed forces as lateral entrants, thereby encountering disadvantages in terms of personnel development, as evidenced by several instances. - A Bundeswehr that is also used to looking to the future could also develop political positions from within itself that could challenge the monopoly of interpretation of politics.

Politicians and generals find it more convenient to lead soldiers who merely pretend foresight and civic engagement.

The trajectory towards the conclusion of the pre-Socratic age in the realm of Inner Leadership appears to have been delineated. The journey involves moving away from the *dichotomous and rigid mindset* of a soldier trained in geometrically structured thinking, towards a *more nuanced and balanced understanding*, with the ultimate goal of accessing the essence - the soul - of a democratic military organization. The concept of identity as discussed by Hegel and other similar thinkers will be of significance in this context. Drawing upon the insights of Clausewitz, such perspectives may not be alien to members of the Bundeswehr. The principles of military strategy and the process of

---

[148] Op. cit. Gadamer. p. 40.

integrating and prioritizing thoughts in Inner Leadership stem from a shared mindset among soldiers.

The dichotomy between cause and effect is no longer the primary framework for thinking and comprehending; the crucial aspect is in what Wilhelm Dilthey (1833-1911), among others, referred to as "Interdependence".[149] The phenomenon at hand is not solely governed by the principles of cause and effect, but rather by a multitude of nuances that collectively give rise to a *rational* progression and *harmonious* composition. Within the framework of the Bundeswehr, this phenomenon may be referred to as a "leadership process" encompassing all the principles outlined in the axioms, hence resulting in the attainment of mission readiness and the accomplishment of missions. Dilthey's suggestion to conceptualize the process of effecting as a melody can draw one's focus towards the sophisticated dynamics of effective leadership exhibited by a competent and authoritative superior. It is evident that this phenomenon possesses an artistic quality that encompasses the harmonious juxtaposition of contrasting elements, rendering it visually and experientially captivating. The phenomenon of trust in a leader resulting from the aforementioned leadership process requires no more elucidation. Therefore, it can be concluded that Inner Leadership plays a crucial role in *enabling the successful achievement of a task*. In the absence of trust in leadership, the endeavor becomes ineffectual and devoid of optimism.

The execution of the mandate should not be situated within a democratic grey area, as emphasized by de Maizière and the concept of the "paradox of the soldier's profession." This paradox highlights the notion that the defense of freedom may require the use of ostensibly undemocratic methods, including the application of force. The existence of this paradox is limited to the realm of bipolar thinking, as opposed to thinking in terms of causal relationships.

An endeavor was undertaken to introduce comprehensiveness and conceptualization into the realm of Inner Leadership through the utilization of axioms. The axioms can be regarded as a "narrative" of significance due to their logical foundation rooted in the rhetoric of Blaise Pascal, warranting serious consideration. This paper focuses on the concept of Inner Leadership as a *vital component within the Bundeswehr*. The commonly employed trio of head, heart, and hand is indeed valid. The Bundeswehr comprises the highest-ranking military officials who provide strategic guidance, skilled personnel who carry out various tasks proficiently, including weapon handling, and a central spirit that imbues purpose into all endeavors, shaping the mindset

---

[149] Cf. also op. cit. Gadamer, p. 28.

and maintaining a steadfast focus on the welfare of the individuals we collectively serve.

For the Bundeswehr to function effectively, it is necessary to possess a comprehensive understanding of law, which regrettably has been largely lost to us, with only limited foundations found in canon law. The military has developed a tendency to consistently advocate for the implementation of novel regulations across several domains, thereby imposing constraints upon itself over an extended period and consequently impeding the attainment of both autonomy and resilience. This perspective is driven by a sense of apprehension towards assuming accountability, with the aim of circumventing the potential reduction of professional prospects. Individuals are generally disinclined to endure the personal ramifications resulting from mistaken choices, irrespective of their well-meaning nature. Moreover, an excessive adherence to legal ethics undermines its own purpose, as it deviates from the fundamental principles of ethics that inherently involve the freedom to make choices and decisions. Nevertheless, this perspective is embraced with a receptive mindset, not only within the context of Inner Leadership, but also inside the Bundeswehr as a comprehensive entity. This is primarily due to the recognition that assigning personal blame for these outcomes is not feasible.

However, it is evident that this has a clear consequence: the quality of our collective efforts for the Bundeswehr is deteriorating, thereby undermining both Inner Leadership and operational readiness. Consequently, this poses a significant threat to the defense capability of our nation. - The more rational option concerning Inner Leadership would involve the cultivation of a discerning faculty that has become ingrained as a disposition, one that grounds its actions on a select set of principles and perceives Inner Leadership as a democratic bestowal onto the personnel, enabling them to act based on deep understanding.

Let us exhibit the bravery to grant Inner Leadership the opportunity to fulfill its potential. In light of the aforementioned analysis, it may be inferred that the conclusion drawn from the critique of Inner Leadership is as follows:

From the spirit of democracy, to gain the timeless as a leadership principle, in order to perceive the one in the other via the person of the superior in all its complexity and conflict, values can be developed, which are then justly defended as identity in the other.

Bibliography

Adorno, T. L. (2000). *Negative Dialektik* (10 ed.). Frankfurt: Suhrkamp.

Bald, D. (2005). Die gespaltene Ausrichtung der Bundeswehr. *Sicherheit und Frieden*.

Baudissin, W. W. (2014). *Grundwert Frieden*. (C. F. Rosen, Ed.) Berlin: Miles-Verlag.

Böckenförde, E.-W. (1991). *Recht, Staat, Freiheit*. Frankfurt/Main.

Böckenförde, E.-W. (1992). Demokratie als Verfassungsprinzip. *Staat, Gesellschaft, Freiheit: Studien zur Staatstheorie und zum Verfassungsrecht*.

Bohnert, M. (2017). *Innere Führung auf dem Prüfstand*. Hamburg: Deutscher Veteranen Verlag.

Cicero, M. T. (1986). *De oratore / Vom Redner*. (H. R. Merklin, Trans.) Stuttgart: Merklin, H., Reclam.

Drexl, R., & Kraus, J. (2019). *Nicht einmal bedingt abwehrbereit. Die Bundeswehr zwischen Elitetruppe und Reformruine*. München: FBVerlag.

Fakir, B. (2022). *Zur Dialektik der Inneren Führung*. Neubiberg.

Gadamer, H.-G. (1996). *Der Anfang der Philosophie*. Stuttgart: Reclam.

Gadamer, H.-G. (1999). *Der Anfang des Wissens*. Stuttgart: Reclam.

Görtemaker, M. (1999). *Geschichte der Bundesrepublik Deutschland: von der Gründung bis zur Gegenwart*. München: C.H. Beck.

Graf, T. (2022). Zwischen Anspruch und Wirklichkeit: Wie steht es um die Bündnistreue in der Bevölkerung. (U. e. Hartmann, Ed.) *Jahrbuch Innere Führung 2021/22*.

Hartmann, U. (2007). *Innere Führung. Erfolge und Defizite der Führungsphilosophie für die Bundeswehr*. Berlin: Miles-Verlag.

Hartmann, U. (2018). *Der gute Soldat. Politische Kultur und soldatisches Selbstverständnis heute*. Berlin: Miles-Verlag.

Hartmann, U. (2020). *Offiziersbibliothek Deutschland*. Berlin: Miles-Verlag.

Hegel, G. W. (1981 (1801)). *Differenz des Fichteschen und Schellingschen Systems (kurz: Differenzschrift)*. Leipzig: Reclam.

Hegel, G. W. (1988). *Phänomenologie des Geistes*. Hamburg: Wessels, H.-F. und Clairmont, H. Meiner.

Heraklit. (2007). *Fragmente* (Vol. 14). Zürich und München: Artemis & Winkler.

Holz, N. (2021). *Zurück in die Zukunft: Empfehlungen zur Wiederentdeckung und Weiterentwicklung der Inneren Führung*. BoD–Books on Demand.

Humboldt, W. v. (1980). *Wilhelm von Humboldt - Werke in fünf Bänden. Band I: Schriften zur Anthropologie und Geschichte.* (3, Ed.) Andreas Flitner und Klaus Giel.

Ilsemann, C.-G. v. (1971). *Die Bundeswehr in der Demokratie. Zeit der Inneren .* Hamburg: Decker's Verlag.

Janke, R. (2023). Innere Führung verstehen, gestalten und erleben. *IF 1/23. Zeitschrift für Innere Führung.*

Jermer, H. (2019). *Innere Führung kompakt. Eine Zusammenschau als Lehr- und Lernhilfe.* Berlin: Miles-Verlag .

Kant, I. (1798). *Anthropologie in pragmatischer Hinsicht.* Königsberg .

Kant, I. (1907). Grundlegung zur Metaphysik der Sitten (1781). *Akademieausgabe AA Bd IV.*

Kielmansegg, J.-A. v. (1966). Der deutsche Soldat und der 20. Juli. *Festschrift zum sechzigsten Geburtstag.*

Kielmansegg, J.-A. v. (1971). Einführung des Herausgebers. In C.-G. Ilsemann, *Die Bundeswehr in der Demokratie. Zeit der Inneren Führung.* Hamburg: Decker's Verlag.

Küng, H. (1990). *Projekt weltethos.* München: Piper.

Lange, S. (2020). : Fit für das 21. Jahrhundert: Warum die Konzeption der Inneren Führung eine neue Meistererzählung benötigt. (U. e. Hartmann, Ed.) *Jahrbuch Innere Führung 2020.*

Lévinas, E. (23 Sept. 1998). *Jenseits des Seins oder anders als Sein geschieht (1978)* (2 ed.). (T. Wiemer, Trans.) Freiburg i.Br: Verlag Karl Alber.

Liessmann, K. P. (09.04.2022). In der Tiefe und auf der Höhe der Zeit. *Neue Züricher Zeitung.*

Maiziere, U. d. (1972). *Bekenntnis zum Soldaten. Militärische Führung in unserer Zeit.* Hamburg: R. v. Deckers Verlag.

Maizière, U. d. (1974). *Führen im Frieden.* München: Bernard und Graefe.

Mangold, A. K. (2019, Mai 09). *Das Böckenförde-Diktum.* Retrieved from https://verfassungsblog.de/das-boeckenfoerde-diktum/

Martin, T. (26. September 2022, September 26). Innere Führung zwischen Zeitenwende und Megatrends. *Alumni FüAk online.*

Neitzel, S. (2022). *Deutsche Krieger. Vom Kaiserreich zur Berliner Republik – eine Militärgeschichte.* Berlin: Ullstein.

Pascal, B. (1963). *Die Kunst zu Überzeugen.* Heidelberg: Lambert Schneider.

Pleines, J.-E. (1 Jan. 2002). *Heraklit: Anfängliches Philosophieren (Studienbücher Antike).* Darmstadt: Georg Olms Verlag.

Rapp, C. (1997). *Vorstokratiker.* München: C. H. BECK .

Rautenberg, H.-J., & Wiggershaus, N. (1/1977). Die „Himmeroder Denkschrift" vom Oktober 1950. *Militärgeschichtliche Mitteilungen (MGM)*.

Reeb, H.-J., & Többicke, P. (2003). *Lexikon Innere Führung*. Regensburg/Berlin: Walhalla-Fachverlag.

Rousseau, J.-J. (1993). *Emil oder über die Erziehung (Émile ou de l'éducation, Paris 1762)* (11 ed.). (F. Schöningh, Trans.) Paderborn.

Sarid, Y. (2021). *Siegerin* (3 ed.). (R. Achlama, Trans.) Zürich: Kein & Aber.

Schiller, F. (1993 (1795)). *Über die ästhetische Erziehung des Menschen in einer Reihe von Briefen*. Stuttgart: Reclam.

Schneider, W. (2003). *Deutsch für Kenner. Die neue Stilkunde*. (8 ed.). München/Zürich: Piper.

Schwarzer, A., & Wagenknecht, S. (2023). Manifest für Frieden.

Spiegel online. (25.2.2022). *Bundeswehrsoldaten in Litauen mangelt es an Jacken und Unterwäsche*. Hamburg.

Stauffenberg, B. (n.d.). Teil 2 Porträt General Schneiderhan. www.youtube.com ARD 2009.

Steiniger, A. (1953). *Ein Lebemann als Staatsmann : Der Vicomte de Barras. Arnold Steiniger*. Berlin; Darmstadt: Dt. Buch-Gemeinschaft.

Strack-Zimmermann, M.-A. (2022, Januar 18). Wünsche mir mehr Klarheit und weniger Geschwurbel der Generalität. (T. Jungholt, Interviewer) www.WELT.de.

Verteidigung, B. d. (2008). *Innere Führung. Selbstverständnis und Führungskultur. A-2600/1*. Bonn.

Vico, G. (1979). *Liber Metaphysicus Riposte (1710)*. (S. O. Viechtbauer, Trans.) München: . Wilhelm Fink Verlag.

Vico, G. (1984). *De nostri temporis studiorum ratione. Latein.-dt. Vom Wesen u. Weg d. geistigen Bildung,.* Darmstadt: Wissenschaftl. Buchgesellschaft.

Wagemann, E. (1982). Fortwirkende Impulse für die „Innere Führung". In U. d. Maizière, *Stationen eines Soldatenlebens*. Bonn: Mittler und Sohn .

Wanner, M. (2022). Innere Führung – Philosophie der Streitkräfte oder bloße Anleitung zur Menschenführung? (M. Elbe, Ed.) *Philosophie des Militärs*.

Wanninger, T. (1999). *Bildung und Gemeinsinn: Ein Beitrag zur Pädagogik der Urteilskraft aus der Philosophie des "sensus communis"*. Bayreuth: Bayreuth Univ. Diss.

Wanninger, T. (2022). Mögliche Grundlegung einer erneuerten Inneren Führung für die Bundeswehr. (U. Hartmann, Ed.) *Jahrbuch Innere Führung 2021/22*.

Watzlawick., P., & Jackson, J. H. (2007). *Menschliche Kommunikation. Formen – Störungen – Paradoxien* (Vol. 11). Bern: Verlag Hans Huber.

Wendroth, H. (2022). *Gute Führung - (k)ein Selbstgänger. Kleine Führungshilfe mit praktischen Hinweisen und persönlichen Anmerkungen.* Berlin: Miles-Verlag.

About the author
Thomas Wanninger

Thomas Wanninger, born in 1971 in Regensburg (Germany), is a Lieutenant Colonel (Reservist). In the German Armed Forces, he was a company commander in the Mountain Infantry, worked at the Centre for Inner Leadership, and advised higher command authorities.

Carola Hartmann Miles-Verlag

Jahrbuch Innere Führung (seit 2009)

Uwe Hartmann, Claus von Rosen (Hrsg.), *Jahrbuch Innere Führung 2017. Die Wiederkehr der Verteidigung in Europa und die Zukunft der Bundeswehr,* Berlin 2017.

Uwe Hartmann, Claus von Rosen (Hrsg.), *Jahrbuch Innere Führung 2018. Innere Führung zwischen Aufbruch, Abbau und Abschaffung: Neues denken, Mitgestaltung fördern, Alternativen wagen,* Berlin 2018.

Uwe Hartmann, Claus von Rosen (Hrsg.), *Jahrbuch Innere Führung 2019. Bundeswehr im Aufbruch. Hindernisse von den verteidigungspolitischen Vorstellungen der AFD bis zu den sicherheitspolitischen Meinungen in der Zivilgesellschaft,* Berlin 2019.

Uwe Hartmann, Reinhold Janke, Claus von Rosen (Hrsg.), *Jahrbuch Innere Führung 2020. Zur Weiterentwicklung der Inneren Führung: Themen und Inhalte,* Berlin 2020.

Uwe Hartmann, Reinhold Janke, Claus von Rosen (Hrsg.), *Jahrbuch Innere Führung 2021/22. Ein neues Mindset Landes- und Bündnisverteidigung?,* Berlin 2022.

Sicherheitspolitik

Wolf Graf v. Baudissin, *Grundwert: Frieden in Politik – Strategie – Führung von Streitkräften, herausgegeben von Claus von Rosen,* Berlin 2014.

Dirk Freudenberg, *Theorie des Irregulären – Erscheinungen und Abgrenzungen von Partisanen, Guerillas und Terroristen im Modernen Kleinkrieg sowie Entwicklungstendenzen der Reaktion, (3 Bände),* Berlin 2017.

Markus Reisner, *Robotic Wars – Legitimatorische Grundlagen und Grenzen des Einsatzes von Military Unmanned Systems in modernen Konfliktszenarien,* Berlin 2018.

Helmut Fiedler, *Military Assistance – eine moderne Einsatzart zwischen Anspruch und Wirklichkeit,* Berlin 2019.

Joachim Weber (Hrsg.), *Konfliktraum Arktis. Die Großmächte und der Hohe Norden,* Berlin 2021.

Thomas Jäger, Ralph Thiele (Hrsg.), *Der Politische Islamismus als hybrider Akteur globaler Reichweite. Die liberale demokratische Ordnung muss ihre Resilienz stärken*, Berlin 2021.

Uwe Hartmann, *Die Nato. Mächte und Menschen in der transatlantischen Allianz*, Berlin 2021.

Carsten Rechtien, *Trumps Amerika – Eine geopolitische Revolution? Tradition und Neuausrichtung der US-Außenpolitik in der beginnenden Ära Trump, Berlin 2022.*

Hans-Peter Weinheimer, *Bevölkerungsschutz 2030 – Anleitung zur Überwindung eines "bewährten" Systems*, Berlin 2022.

Militär und Gesellschaft

Marcel Bohnert, Lukas J. Reitstetter (Hrsg.), *Armee im Aufbruch. Zur Gedankenwelt junger Offiziere in den Kampftruppen der Bundeswehr*, Berlin 2014.

Phil C. Langer, Gerhard Kümmel (Hrsg.), *„Wir sind Bundeswehr." Wie viel Vielfalt benötigen/vertragen die Streitkräfte?*, Berlin 2015.

Eberhard Birk, Peter Andreas Popp (Hrsg.), *Luftwaffenoffizier 21. Das Selbstverständnis des Luftwaffenoffiziers zu Beginn des 21. Jahrhunderts, (aus der Reihe Schriften zur Geschichte der Deutschen Luftwaffe, Band 5)*, Berlin 2016.

Alois Bach, Walter Sauer (Hrsg.), *Schützen.Retten.Kämpfen. Dienen für Deutschland*, Berlin 2016.

Marcel Bohnert, Björn Schreiber (Hrsg.), *Die unsichtbaren Veteranen. Kriegsheimkehrer in der deutschen Gesellschaft*, Berlin 2016.

Angelika Dörfler-Dierken (Hrsg.), *Hinschauen! Geschlecht, Rechtspopulismus, Rituale: Systemische Probleme oder individuelles Fehlverhalten?*, Berlin 2019.

Einsatzerfahrungen

Artur Schwitalla, *Afghanistan, jetzt weiß ich erst...*, Berlin 2010.

Sascha Brinkmann, Joachim Hoppe (Hg.), *Generation Einsatz. Fallschirmjäger berichten ihre Erfahrungen aus Afghanistan*, Berlin 2010.

Ingo Werners, *Fahren, Funken, Feuern. Hinweise auf die Einsatzvorbereitung*, Berlin 2010.

Rainer Buske, *KUNDUZ. Ein Erlebnisbericht über einen militärischen Einsatz der Bundeswehr in Afghanistan im Jahre 2008,* Berlin 2015.

Marcel Bohnert, Andy Neumann, *German Mechanized Infantry on Combat Operations in Afghanistan,* Berlin 2016.

Alois Bach, Carola Hartmann (Hrsg.), *Unbekannte Helden des Alltags. Soldaten und Ehefrauen berichten über Verantwortung, Humanität und Belastung im Auslandseinsatz,* Berlin 2020.

Kurt Helmut Schiebold, *99 Tage in Afghanistan. Wie der deutsche Einsatz 2003 im Nordosten Afghanistans begann. Aus meinem Tagebuch,* Berlin 2022.

Christian Gerstner, *Unter dem Schwert. 15 Jahre im Kommando Spezialkräfte,* Berlin 2023.

Militärgeschichte

Eberhard Kliem, Kathrin Orth, *"Wir wurden wie blödsinnig vom Feind beschossen". Menschen und Schiffe in der Skagerrakschlacht 1916,* Berlin 2016.

Hans Frank, Norbert Rath, *Kommodore Rudolf Petersen. Führer der Schnellboote 1942–1945. Ein Leben in Licht und Schatten unteilbarer Verantwortung,* Berlin 2016.

Eckhard Lisec, *Der Völkermord an den Armeniern im 1. Weltkrieg – Deutsche Offiziere beteiligt?,* Berlin 2017.

Ingo Pfeiffer, *Heinz Neukirchen. Marinekarriere an wechselnden Fronten,* Berlin 2017.

Joachim Welz, *Erfolgsstory oder Trauma – die Übernahme von Armeen. Lehren aus der Übernahme des österreichischen Bundesheeres in die Wehrmacht 1938 und der Reste der NVA in die Bundeswehr 1990,* Berlin 2018.

Joachim Hoppe, Manfred Wilde (Hrsg.), *Die Unteroffizierschule des Heeres, Die militärische Meisterschule,* Berlin 2016.

Georg Neuhaus, *Am Anfang war ein Speer. Eine Chronographie der Kriegs- und Militärtechnologien,* Berlin 2018.

Hans-Werner Ahrens, *Die Transportflieger der Luftwaffe 1956 bis 1971. Konzeption – Aufbau – Einsatz, (Reihe Schriften zur Geschichte der Deutschen Luftwaffe, Band 8),* Berlin 2019.

Jobst Reller, *Die Anfänge der evangelischen Militärseelsorge,* Berlin ²2020.

Eberhard Frhr. v. Senden, Friedrich Frhr. v. Senden, *Der Erste Weltkrieg 1914–1918. Erlebnisse eines jungen Leutnants,* Berlin 2020.

Hans-Günter Behrendt, *Flugabwehr in Deutschland. Stationierungsorte und Systeme 1956-2012,* Berlin 2021.

Harald Fritz Potempa, *Balkan 1914-1945. Raum und Kleiner Krieg als militärhistorische Kategorien in der Wahrnehmung deutscher Streitkräfte,* Berlin 2021.

Stephan Horn, *Französische und wallonische Freiwilligenverbände im Zweiten Weltkrieg. Politische Implikationen militärischer Kollaboration,* Berlin 2021.

Jörg Beining, *Streng geheim! Elektronische Kampfführung im Kalten Krieg. Die EloKa der Bundeswehr und NATO aus östlicher Perspektive,* Berlin 2021.

Gerd Bolik, *NATO-Planungen für die Verteidigung der Bundesrepublik Deutschland im Kalten Krieg,* Berlin 2021.

Martin Kutz, *Die Schlacht als Männerballett oder Mythos und Militär,* Berlin 2022.

Olaf Rönnau, *Eine totale Institution als Zwischenspiel. Die Kadettenschule der NVA von ihrer Gründung 1956 bis zu ihrer Auflösung 1961,* Berlin 2022.

Stephan Maninger, *Für einige Morgen aus Eis und Schnee – Großbritanniens Kampf um Nordamerika 1754-1763,* Berlin 2022.

Olaf Rönnau, *Oberst Franz Weller (1901-1994) vom Kadettenkorps zur Bundeswehr. Soldat in drei Armeen. Erinnerungen an den ersten Kommandeur Infanterieschule Hammelburg (1956-1957),* Berlin 2023.

Erinnerungen

Blue Braun, *Erinnerungen an die Marine 1956–1996,* Berlin 2012.

Rainer Buske, *Eine Reise ins Innere der Bundeswehr. Wundersame Geschichten aus einer anderen Welt,* Berlin 2016.

Heinz Laube, *Duell am Himmel,* Berlin 2016.

Viktor Toyka, *Dienst in Zeiten des Wandels. Erinnerungen aus 40 Jahren Dienst als Marineoffizier 1966-2000,* Berlin 2017.

Hans-Eckhard Tribess (Hrsg.), *Im Leben unterwegs – für den Frieden. Festschrift für Wolfgang Altenburg zum 90. Geburtstag am 22. Juni 2018,* Berlin 2019.

Kurt Graf v. Schweinitz, *Notizen im Transit von Krieg und Frieden,* Berlin 2020.

Karl-Otto Behrendt, *Der kurze Bericht über eine lange Zeit. Kriegsgefangenschaft 1945–1953, herausgegeben und kommentiert von Hans-Günter Behrendt,* Berlin 2021.

Hans Peter von Kirchbach, *Herz an der Angel,* Berlin 2021.

Dieter Wolf, *Erlebnisse eines MAD-Offiziers und Leistungssportlers,* Berlin 2022.

Klaus Beckmann, *Dienstweg –kein Durchgang? Als Pfarrer und Staatsbürger in der Bundeswehr,* Berlin 2022.

Bernhard R. Kroener, *Lebensscherben –Hoffnungsspuren. Eine Familie aus Schlesien in den Stürmen des 20. Jahrhundert. In zwei Bänden. Eine dokumentarische Erzählung. Mit einer Familienstammfolge von Peter Bahl,* Berlin 2023.

Schriften zur Tradition

Eberhard Birk, Winfried Heinemann, Sven Lange (Hrsg.), *Tradition für die Bundeswehr. Neue Aspekte einer alten Debatte,* Berlin 2012.

Donald Abenheim, Uwe Hartmann (Hrsg.), *Tradition in der Bundeswehr. Zum Erbe des deutschen Soldaten und zur Umsetzung des neuen Traditionserlasses,* Berlin 2018.

Joachim Welz, *Vom Kontingentsheer zum Reichsheer: Militärkonventionen als Motor der Wehrverfassung,* Berlin 2018.

Donald Abenheim, Uwe Hartmann, *Einführung in die Tradition der Bundeswehr. Das soldatische Erbe in dem besten Deutschland, das es je gab,* Berlin 2019.

Eberhard Birk, Heiner Möllers (Hrsg.), *Die Luftwaffe und ihre Traditionen (aus der Reihe Schriften zur Geschichte der Deutschen Luftwaffe, Band 10),* Berlin 2019.

Hans-Günter Behrendt (Hrsg.): *Erinnerungsorte der Bundeswehr – Personen, Ereignisse und Institutionen der soldatischen Traditionspflege,* Berlin 2020.

Dirk Drews, Stefan Gruhl (Hrsg.): *Oberst Reinhard Hauschild 1921–2005. Traditionsstifter für die Bundeswehr? Gedenkschrift zum 100. Geburtstag,* Berlin 2021.

Dieter Krüger, *Verständigung mit Frankreich. Das vergebliche Plädoyer des Oberst Dr. Hans Speidel. Paris 1940–1942,* Berlin 2021.

Martin Kutz, *Besuch im Soldatenhimmel. Ein wissenschaftlicher Reisebericht aus einer anderen Welt,* Berlin 2022.

Standpunkte und Orientierungen

Uwe Hartmann (Hrsg.), *Lernen von Afghanistan. Innovative Mittel und Wege für Auslandseinsätze,* Berlin 2015.

Uwe Hartmann, *Hybrider Krieg als neue Bedrohung von Freiheit und Frieden. Zur Relevanz der Inneren Führung in Politik, Gesellschaft und Streitkräften,* Berlin 2015.

Hartwig von Schubert, *Integrative Militärethik. Ethische Urteilsbildung in der militärischen Führung,* Berlin 2015.

Martin Sebaldt, *Nicht abwehrbereit. Die Kardinalprobleme der deutschen Streitkräfte, der Offenbarungseid des Weißbuchs und die Wege aus der Gefahr,* Berlin 2017.

Uwe Hartmann, *Der gute Soldat. Politische Kultur und soldatisches Selbstverständnis heute,* Berlin 2018.

Helmut Jermer, *Innere Führung kompakt. Eine Zusammenschau als Lehr- und Lernhilfe,* Berlin 2019.

Martin Sebaldt, *Das Elend der Strategen. Warum die deutsche Militärpolitik versagt,* Berlin 2020.

Hannes Wendroth, *Gute Führung – (k)ein Selbstgänger. Kleine Führungshilfe mit praktischen Hinweisen und persönlichen Anmerkungen,* Berlin 2022.

Hans-Christian Witthauer, Thomas Saller, *Führung und das 3 Alpha Prinzip. Militärisches Handwerkszeug für den zivilen Führungsalltag,* Berlin 2023.

www.miles-verlag.jimdo.com